D1360419

EVERYMAN,
I WILL GO WITH THEE
AND BE THY GUIDE,
IN THY MOST NEED
TO GO BY THY SIDE

WITHDRAWN

EVERYMAN'S LIBRARY
POCKET POETS

VILLA JULIE COLLEGE LIBRARY
STEVENSON MD 21153

War Poems

Selected and edited by
John Hollander

EVERYMAN'S LIBRARY

POCKET POETS

Alfred A. Knopf · New York · Toronto

THIS IS A BORZOI BOOK
PUBLISHED BY ALFRED A. KNOPF

This selection by John Hollander first published in
Everyman's Library, 1999

Copyright © 1999 by David Campbell Publishers Ltd.

Second printing

A list of acknowledgments to copyright owners can be found at the back of
this volume.

All rights reserved under International and Pan-American Copyright
Conventions. Published in the United States by Alfred A. Knopf, a division
of Random House, Inc., New York, and simultaneously in Canada by
Random House of Canada Limited, Toronto. Distributed by Random
House, Inc., New York

www.randomhouse.com/everymans

ISBN 0-375-40790-1

Library of Congress Cataloging-in-Publication Data
War poems / selected and edited by John Hollander.
p.   cm.—(Everyman's library pocket poets)
ISBN 0-375-40790-1 (hc : alk. paper)
1. War Poetry.   I. Hollander. John.   II. Series.
PN6110.W28W37   1999   99-36043
808.81'9358—dc21   CIP

Typography by Peter B. Willberg
Typeset in the UK by AccComputing, North Barrow, Somerset
Printed and bound in Germany by GGP Media, Pössneck

CONTENTS

BEFORE AND AFTER NAPOLEON

THE AMERICAN CIVIL WAR

MODERN WARFARE: WORLD WAR I

8

GENERAL OBSERVATIONS

FOREWORD

"I was going to hold forth on arms, and the violence of warfare, in a meter suited to the matter," wrote the Roman poet Ovid at the start of a collection of erotic poems (the meter would have been the heroic hexameters of Virgil's *Aeneid*), "but Cupid, laughing," he continued, "stole one foot from the second line" – thus turning the meter into the elegiac couplets, each with a second pentameter, appropriate to love poetry. Ovid's little joke acknowledges that in antiquity the battlefield, rather than the bed, was considered a more fitting subject for literary treatment; certainly many of the oldest poetic texts we have include tales of combat. The actualities of armed conflict – weapons, scope, scale, logistics and tactics, the relation of fighters to non-combatants – have undergone many changes since Ovid mischievously failed to write his military epic. So, too, have the linguistic materials, structures and rhetorical intentions of poetry itself. But while Cupid may now have more troops in the field than Mars, poets today and throughout the ages have never ceased to write about war.

In the diversity of the poetry over which they may be said to preside, Mars and Cupid have turned out to be pretty evenly matched. Over the centuries, war has evoked a whole range of moods other than the strictly martial. War poetry may express sorrow, hope, despair, prophetic vision, moral and philosophical reflection; it may even trespass upon Cupid's own domain of love. It can strike a resounding note of triumph, pride or patriotism, or adopt a subdued tone of loss and regret. Where one poem is unashamedly belligerent in spirit, another is compassionate, another ironic. Where one poet is passionately engaged, another observes with detachment. Military glory is both extolled and execrated. The fallen are commemorated as heroes, or mourned as victims. There is horror and disgust, bitterness, fascination, even wry amusement. There is often a sense of tragedy but there may sometimes be a touch of comedy as well. In my selection, organized chronologically to chart changing attitudes to war, I have sought to represent this tremendously varied response to an age-old human theme.

JOHN HOLLANDER

I should like to acknowledge the wise assistance of my student Aidan Wasley in preparing this anthology.

WAR POEMS

HEROIC AGES:
ANCIENT THROUGH
RENAISSANCE

THE WAR IN HEAVEN: RAPHAEL TELLS
OF SATAN'S ARTILLERY

So scoffing in ambiguous words he scarce
Had ended; when to right and left the front
Divided, and to either flank retired.
Which to our eyes discovered new and strange,
A triple mounted row of pillars laid
On wheels (for like to pillars most they seemed
Or hollowed bodies made of oak or fir,
With branches lopped, in wood or mountain felled)
Brass, iron, stony mould, had not their mouths
With hideous orifice gaped on us wide,
Portending hollow truce; at each behind
A seraph stood, and in his hand a reed
Stood waving tipped with fire; while we suspense,
Collected stood within our thoughts amused,
Not long, for sudden all at once their reeds
Put forth, and to a narrow vent applied
With nicest touch. Immediate in a flame,
But soon obscured with smoke, all heaven appeared,
From those deep throated engines belched, whose roar
Embowelled with outrageous noise the air,
And all her entrails tore, disgorging foul
Their devilish glut, chained thunderbolts and hail
Or iron globes, which on the victor host
Levelled, with such impetuous fury smote,

That whom they hit, none on their feet might stand,
Though standing else as rocks, but down they fell
By thousands, angel on archangel rolled . . .

DAVID'S LAMENT OVER SAUL AND JONATHAN

The beauty of Israel is slain upon thy high places: how
    are the mighty fallen!
Tell it not in Gath, publish it not in the streets of
    Askelon; lest the daughters of the Philistines
    rejoice, lest the daughters of the uncircumcised
    triumph.
Ye mountains of Gilboa, let there be no dew, neither
    let there be rain, upon you, nor fields of offerings:
    for there the shield of the mighty is vilely cast
    away, the shield of Saul, as though he had not been
    anointed with oil.
From the blood of the slain, from the fat of the mighty,
    the bow of Jonathan turned not back, and the
    sword of Saul returned not empty.
Saul and Jonathan were lovely and pleasant in their
    lives, and in their death they were not divided:
    they were swifter than eagles, they were stronger
    than lions.
Ye daughters of Israel, weep over Saul, who clothed
    you in scarlet, with other delights, who put on
    ornaments of gold upon your apparel.
How are the mighty fallen in the midst of the battle! O
    Jonathan, thou wast slain in thine high places.

I am distressed for thee, my brother Jonathan: very
     pleasant hast thou been unto me: thy love to me
     was wonderful, passing the love of women.
How are the mighty fallen, and the weapons of war
     perished!

THE DESTRUCTION OF SENNACHERIB

The Assyrian came down like the wolf on the fold,
And his cohorts were gleaming in purple and gold;
And the sheen of their spears was like stars on the sea,
When the blue wave rolls nightly on deep Galilee.

Like the leaves of the forest when Summer is green,
That host with their banners at sunset were seen:
Like the leaves of the forest when Autumn hath blown,
That host on the morrow lay withered and strown.

For the Angel of Death spread his wings on the blast,
And breathed in the face of the foe as he passed;
And the eyes of the sleepers waxed deadly and chill,
And their hearts but once heaved, and for ever
        grew still!

And there lay the steed with his nostril all wide,
But through it there rolled not the breath of his pride:
And the foam of his gasping lay white on the turf,
And cold as the spray of the rock-beating surf.

And there lay the rider distorted and pale,
With the dew on his brow, and the rust on his mail;
And the tents were all silent, the banners alone,
The lances unlifted, the trumpet unblown.

And the widows of Ashur are loud in their wail,
And the idols are broke in the temple of Baal;
And the might of the Gentile, unsmote by the sword,
Hath melted like snow in the glance of the Lord!

ACHILLES OVER THE TRENCH
from the Iliad

Then rose Achilles dear to Zeus; and round
The warrior's puissant shoulders Pallas flung
Her fringèd ægis, and around his head
The glorious goddess wreathed a golden cloud,
And from it lighted an all-shining flame.
As when a smoke from a city goes to heaven
Far off from out an island girt by foes,
All day the men contend in grievous war
From their own city, but with set of sun
Their fires flame thickly, and aloft the glare
Flies streaming, if perchance the neighbours round
May see, and sail to help them in the war;
So from his head the splendour went to heaven.
From wall to dyke he stept, he stood, nor joined
The Achæans – honouring his wise mother's word –
There standing, shouted, and Pallas far away
Called; and a boundless panic shook the foe.
For like the clear voice when a trumpet shrills,
Blown by the fierce beleaguerers of a town,
So rang the clear voice of Æakidês;
And when the brazen cry of Æakidês
Was heard among the Trojans, all their hearts
Were troubled, and the full-maned horses whirled
The chariots backward, knowing griefs at hand;

23

And sheer-astounded were the charioteers
To see the dread, unweariable fire
That always o'er the great Peleion's head
Burned, for the bright-eyed goddess made it burn.
Thrice from the dyke he sent his mighty shout,
Thrice backward reeled the Trojans and allies;
And there and then twelve of their noblest died
Among their spears and chariots.

TRANSLATED BY ALFRED, LORD TENNYSON

A PAUSE IN THE FIGHTING
from the Iliad

So Hector spake; the Trojans roared applause;
Then loosed their sweating horses from the yoke,
And each beside his chariot bound his own;
And oxen from the city, and goodly sheep
In haste they drove, and honey-hearted wine
And bread from out the houses brought, and heaped
Their firewood, and the winds from off the plain
Rolled the rich vapour far into the heaven.
And these all night upon the bridge of war
Sat glorying; many a fire between them blazed:
As when in heaven the stars about the moon
Look beautiful, when all the winds are laid,
And every height comes out, and jutting peak
And valley, and the immeasurable heavens
Break open to their highest, and all the stars
Shine, and the Shepherd gladdens in his heart:
So many a fire between the ships and stream
Of Xanthus blazed before the towers of Troy,
A thousand on the plain; and close by each
Sat fifty in the blaze of burning fire;
And eating hoary grain and pulse the steeds,
Fixt by their cars, waited the golden dawn.

HOMER   25
TRANSLATED BY ALFRED, LORD TENNYSON

BALLAD OF HECTOR IN HADES

Yes, this is where I stood that day,
    Beside this sunny mound.
The walls of Troy are far away,
    And outward comes no sound.

I wait. On all the empty plain
    A burnished stillness lies,
Save for the chariot's tinkling hum,
    And a few distant cries.

His helmet glitters near. The world
    Slowly turns around,
With some new sleight compels my feet
    From the fighting ground.

I run. If I turned back again
    The earth must turn with me,
The mountains planted on the plain,
    The sky clamped to the sea.

The grasses puff a little dust
    Where my footsteps fall.
I cast a shadow as I pass
    The little wayside wall.

The strip of grass on either hand
    Sparkles in the light;
I only see that little space
    To the left and to the right,

And in that space our shadows run,
    His shadow there and mine,
The little flowers, the tiny mounds,
    The grasses frail and fine.

But narrower still and narrower!
    My course is shrunk and small,
Yet vast as in a deadly dream,
    And faint the Trojan wall.
The sun up in the towering sky
    Turns like a spinning ball.

The sky with all its clustered eyes
    Grows still with watching me,
The flowers, the mounds, the flaunting weeds
    Wheel slowly round to see.

Two shadows racing on the grass,
    Silent and so near,
Until his shadow falls on mine.
    And I am rid of fear.

The race is ended. Far away
   I hang and do not care,
While round bright Troy Achilles whirls
   A corpse with streaming hair.

CÆSAR CROSSES THE RUBICON
from Pharsalia

    Cæsar has crossed the Alps, his mighty soul
Great tumults pondering and the coming shock.
Now on the marge of Rubicon, he saw,
In face most sorrowful and ghostly guise,
His trembling country's image; huge it seemed
Through mists of night obscure; and hoary hair
Streamed from the lofty front with turrets crowned:
Torn were her locks and naked were her arms.
Then thus, with broken sighs the Vision spake:
"What seek ye, men of Rome? and whither hence
Bear ye my standards? If by right ye come,
My citizens, stay here; these are the bounds;
No further dare." But Cæsar's hair was stiff
With horror as he gazed, and ghastly dread
Restrained his footsteps on the further bank.
Then spake he, "Thunderer, who from the rock
Tarpeian seest the wall of mighty Rome;
Gods of my race who watched o'er Troy of old;
Thou Jove of Alba's height, and Vestal fires,
And rites of Romulus erst rapt to heaven,
And God-like Rome; be friendly to my quest.
Not with offence or hostile arms I come,
Thy Cæsar, conqueror by land and sea,
Thy soldier here and wheresoe'er thou wilt:

No other's; his, his only be the guilt
Whose acts make me thy foe." He gives the word
And bids his standards cross the swollen stream.
So in the wastes of Afric's burning clime
The lion crouches as his foes draw near,
Feeding his wrath the while, his lashing tail
Provokes his fury; stiff upon his neck
Bristles his mane: deep from his gaping jaws
Resounds the muttered growl, and should a lance
Or javelin reach him from the hunter's ring,
Scorning the puny scratch he bounds afield.

From modest fountain blood-red Rubicon
In summer's heat flows on; his pigmy tide
Creeps through the valleys and with slender marge
Divides the Italian peasant from the Gaul.
Then winter gave him strength, and fraught with rain
The third day's crescent moon; while Eastern winds
Thawed from the Alpine slopes the yielding snow.
The cavalry first form across the stream
To break the torrent's force; the rest with ease
Beneath their shelter gain the further bank.
When Cæsar crossed and trod beneath his feet
The soil of Italy's forbidden fields,
"Here," spake he, "peace, here broken laws be left;
Farewell to treaties. Fortune, lead me on;
War is our judge, and in the fates our trust."
Then in the shades of night he leads the troops

Swifter than Balearic sling or shaft
Winged by retreating Parthian, to the walls
Of threatened Rimini, while fled the stars,
Save Lucifer, before the coming sun,
Whose fires were veiled in clouds, by south wind
    driven,
Or else at heaven's command: and thus drew on
The first dark morning of the civil war.

GO TELL THE SPARTANS

Go tell the Spartans, thou that passest by,
That here obedient to their laws we lie.

SIMONIDES

TRANSLATED BY WILLIAM LISLE BOWLES

ÆNEAS KILLS TURNUS
from the Æneid

    Now stern Æneas waves his weighty spear
Against his foe, and thus upbraids his fear:
"What farther subterfuge can Turnus find?
What empty hopes are harboured in his mind?
'Tis not thy swiftness can secure thy flight;
Not with their feet, but hands, the valiant fight.
Vary thy shape in thousand forms, and dare
What skill and courage can attempt in war:
Wish for the wings of winds, to mount the sky;
Or hid within the hollow earth to lie!"
The champion shook his head, and made this
      short reply:
"No threats of thine my manly mind can move;
'Tis hostile heaven I dread, and partial Jove."
He said no more, but, with a sigh, repressed
The mighty sorrow in his swelling breast.
Then, as he rolled his troubled eyes around,
An antique stone he saw, the common bound
Of neighbouring fields, and barrier of the ground –
So vast, that twelve strong men of modern days
The enormous weight from earth could hardly raise.
He heaved it at a lift, and, poised on high,
Ran staggering on against his enemy;
But so disordered, that he scarcely knew

His way, or what unwieldy weight he threw.
His knocking knees are bent beneath the load;
And shivering cold congeals his vital blood.
The stone drops from his arms, and, falling short
For want of vigour, mocks his vain effort.
And as, when heavy sleep has closed the sight,
The sickly fancy labours in the night;
We seem to run; and, destitute of force,
Our sinking limbs forsake us in the course:
In vain we heave for breath; in vain we cry:
The nerves, unbraced, their usual strength deny;
And on the tongue the faltering accents die:
So Turnus fared: whatever means he tried,
All force of arms, and points of art employed,
The Fury flew athwart, and made the endeavour void.

    A thousand various thoughts his soul confound:
He stared about, nor aid nor issue found:
His own men stop the pass, and his own walls
      surround.
Once more he pauses, and looks out again,
And seeks the goddess charioteer in vain.
Trembling he views the thundering chief advance,
And brandishing aloft the deadly lance:
Amazed he cowers beneath his conquering foe,
Forgets to ward, and waits the coming blow.
Astonished while he stands, and fixed with fear,
Aimed at his shield he sees the impending spear.

The hero measured first, with narrow view,
The destined mark; and, rising as he threw,
With its full swing the fatal weapon flew.
Not with less rage the rattling thunder falls,
Or stones from battering engines break the walls:
Swift as a whirlwind, from an arm so strong,
The lance drove on, and bore the death along.
Nought could his sevenfold shield the prince avail,
Nor aught, beneath his arms, the coat of mail;
It pierced through all, and with a grisly wound
Transfixed his thigh, and doubled him to ground.
With groans the Latins rend the vaulted sky:
Woods, hills, and valleys, to the voice reply.
    Now low on earth the lofty chief is laid,
With eyes cast upwards, and with arms displayed,
And, recreant, thus to the proud victor prayed:
"I know my death deserved, nor hope to live:
Use what the gods and thy good fortune give.
Yet think, oh think! if mercy may be shown,
(Thou hadst a father once, and hast a son),
Pity my sire, now sinking to the grave;
And, for Anchises' sake, old Daunus save!
Or, if thy vowed revenge pursue my death,
Give to my friends my body void of breath!
The Latian chiefs have seen me beg my life:
Thine is the conquest, thine the royal wife:
Against a yielded man, 'tis mean ignoble strife."

In deep suspense the Trojan seemed to stand,
And, just prepared to strike, repressed his hand.
He rolled his eyes, and every moment felt
His manly soul with more compassion melt;
When, casting down a casual glance, he spied
The golden belt that glittered on his side,
The fatal spoil which haughty Turnus tore
From dying Pallas, and in triumph wore.
Then, roused anew to wrath, he loudly cries
(Flames, while he spoke, came flashing from his eyes),
"Traitor! dost thou, dost thou to grace pretend,
Clad, as thou art, in trophies of my friend?
To his sad soul a grateful offering go!
'Tis Pallas, Pallas gives this deadly blow."
He raised his arm aloft, and, at the word,
Deep in his bosom drove the shining sword.
The streaming blood distained his arms around;
And the disdainful soul came rushing through
      the wound.

TRANSLATED BY JOHN DRYDEN

ÆNEAS TELLS OF THE TROJAN HORSE
from the Æneid

By destiny compell'd, and in despair,
The Greeks grew weary of the tedious war,
And by Minerva's aid a fabric rear'd,
Which like a steed of monstrous height appear'd:
The sides were plank'd with pine; they feign'd it made
For their return, and this the vow they paid
Thus they pretend, but in the hollow side
Selected numbers of their soldiers hide:
With inward arms the dire machine they load,
And iron bowels stuff the dark abode.
In sight of Troy lies Tenedos, an isle
(While Fortune did on Priam's empire smile)
Renown'd for wealth; but, since, a faithless bay,
Where ships expos'd to wind and weather lay.
There was their fleet conceal'd. We thought,
    for Greece
Their sails were hoisted, and our fears release.
The Trojans, coop'd within their walls so long,
Unbar their gates, and issue in a throng,
Like swarming bees, and with delight survey
The camp deserted, where the Grecians lay:
The quarters of the sev'ral chiefs they show'd;
Here Phœnix, here Achilles, made abode;
Here join'd the battles; there the navy rode.

Part on the pile their wond'ring eyes employ:
The pile by Pallas rais'd to ruin Troy.
Thymœtes first ('tis doubtful whether hir'd,
Or so the Trojan destiny requir'd)
Mov'd that the ramparts might be broken down,
To lodge the monster fabric in the town.
But Capys, and the rest of sounder mind,
The fatal present to the flames design'd,
Or to the wat'ry deep; at least to bore
The hollow sides, and hidden frauds explore.
The giddy vulgar, as their fancies guide,
With noise say nothing, and in parts divide.
Laocoon, follow'd by a num'rous crowd,
Ran from the fort, and cried, from far, aloud:
"O wretched countrymen! what fury reigns?
What more than madness has possess'd your brains?
Think you the Grecians from your coasts are gone?
And are Ulysses' arts no better known?
This hollow fabric either must inclose,
Within its blind recess, our secret foes;
Or 'tis an engine rais'd above the town,
T' o'erlook the walls, and then to batter down.
Somewhat is sure design'd, by fraud or force:
Trust not their presents, nor admit the horse."
Thus having said, against the steed he threw
His forceful spear, which, hissing as it flew,
Pierc'd thro' the yielding planks of jointed wood,

And trembling in the hollow belly stood.
The sides, transpierc'd, return a rattling sound,
And groans of Greeks inclos'd come issuing thro'
    the wound.
And, had not Heav'n the fall of Troy design'd,
Or had not men been fated to be blind,
Enough was said and done t' inspire a better mind.
Then had our lances pierc'd the treach'rous wood,
And Ilian tow'rs and Priam's empire stood.

DULCE ET DECORUM EST
PRO PATRIA MORI

Disciplined in the school of hard campaigning,
Let the young Roman study how to bear
Rigorous difficulties without complaining,
And camp with danger in the open air,

And with his horse and lance become the scourge of
Wild Parthians. From the ramparts of the town
Of the warring king, the princess on the verge of
Womanhood with her mother shall look down

And sigh: "Ah, royal lover, still a stranger
To battle, do not recklessly excite
That lion, savage to touch, whom murderous anger
Drives headlong through the thickest of the fight."

The glorious and the decent way of dying
Is for one's country. Run, and death will seize
You no less surely. The young coward, flying,
Get his quietus in the back and knees.

Unconscious of mere loss of votes and shining
With honours that the mob's breath cannot dim,
True worth is not found raising or resigning
The fasces at the breeze of popular whim.

For those who do not merit death, exploring
Ways barred to ordinary men, true worth
Opens a path to heaven and spurns on soaring
Pinions the trite crowds and the clogging earth.

Trusty discretion too shall be rewarded
Duly. I will not suffer a tell-tale
Of Ceres' sacred mysteries to be boarded
Under my roof or let my frail boat sail

With him; for, slighted, often God confuses
The innocent with the evil-doer's fate.
Yet Vengeance, with one lame foot, seldom loses
Track of the outlaw, though she sets off late.

HORACE   41
TRANSLATED BY JAMES MICHIE

AFTER THE BATTLE OF ACTIUM

I rejoice with you in the triumph of Cæsar,
    Mæcenas. How soon shall we drink
the Cæcuban put aside for celebrations
    beneath your high roof, as Jove smiles,
and the flute and the lyre join in a medley of
    Dorian and Phrygian songs?
As we did when Pompey, that son of Neptune, fled,
    driven from the sea, his ships burned,
for all that he threatened our city with the chains
    of the runaway slaves, his friends.
A Roman, ah god, – will times to come believe it? –
    a slave to a woman's orders,
bears his weapons and stakes, a soldier who can stand
    to serve under wrinkled eunuchs,
and the sun sees the shame of oriental tents
    in the midst of army banners.   ⌈mounts
One look at this, and two thousand Gauls turned their
    the other way, crying "Cæsar,"
and the enemy ships, commanded to sail left,
    turned sterns and hid in the harbor.
Hail, God of Triumph! Why not bring out the golden
    chariots and the unyoked bulls?
Hail, God of Triumph! No general equals him,
    not the one who fought Jugurtha,

not Africanus, whose courage raised for him
    a monument over Carthage.
Beaten by land and sea, the enemy changes
    his scarlet mantle to mourning,
and scurries towards Crete, famed for its hundred cities
    (the winds are not in his favor),
or towards the Syrtes that are tossed by the Southwind,
    or he steers an uncertain course.
Boy, bring the larger goblets over here to us
    and Chian wine, or Lesbian;
better still, keep our seasickness under control
    by pouring us some Cæcuban.
It is good to shake off fears and worries for Cæsar
    with the joys of carefree Bacchus.

THE EVILS OF WAR

How evil a thing is War, that bows men to shameful
      rest!
War burns away in her blaze all glory and boasting
      of men:
Nought stands but the valiant heart to face pain, the
      hardhoofed steed,
The ring-mail set close and firm, the nail-crowned
      helms and the spears,
And onset again after rout, when men shrink from the
      serried array –
Then, then, fall away all the vile, the hirelings, and
      Shame is strong!
War girds up her skirts before them, and Evil unmixed
      is bare.
For their hearts were for maidens veiled, not for
      driving the gathered spoil:
Yea, evil the heirs we leave, sons of Yashkur and
      al-Laḳâḥ!

But let flee her fires who will, no flinching for me,
      son of Ḳais!
O children of Ḳais, stand firm before her, gain peace
      or give:
Who seeks flight before her fear, his Doom stands
      and bars the road.

Away! Death allows no quitting of place, and brands
    are bare!
What is life for us when the Uplands and valleys are
    ours no more?
Ah, where are the mighty now, the spears and the
    generous hands?

ANON., ARABIC 7TH CENTURY   45
TRANSLATED BY CHARLES JAMES LYALL

FIRST WAR

First war resembles
   a beautiful mouth we
all want to flirt with
    and believe –.

Later it's more
   a repulsive old whore
whose callers are bitter
    and grieve.

     TRANSLATED BY PETER COLE

ALAS FOR US SOLDIERS

What plant is not faded?
What day do we not march?
What man is not taken
To defend the four bounds?

What plant is not wilting?
What man is not taken from his wife?
Alas for us soldiers,
Treated as though we were not fellow-men!

Are we buffaloes, are we tigers
That our home should be these desolate wilds?
Alas for us soldiers,
Neither by day nor night can we rest!

The fox bumps and drags
Through the tall, thick grass.
Inch by inch move our barrows
As we push them along the track.

ANON., CHINESE
TRANSLATED BY ARTHUR WALEY

A RIDDLE

Injured by iron   I am a loner
Scarred by the strokes   of the sword's edge
Wearied of battle.   War I behold
The fiercest foes   yet I hope for no help
No comfort for me   to come out of battle
Before among people   I perish completely
But the keen swords   skilfully forged,
The handiwork hard-edged   of hammering smiths,
Bite into my stronghold.   I must ever abide
An encounter more dire;   never a doctor
Will I ever find   on the field of fighting
To heal with herbs   the grievous hurts,
But my sword-wounds   are ever widened
By death-blows dealt me   day and night.

[Answer: *Shield*]

LAMENT OF THE FRONTIER GUARD

By the North Gate, the wind blows full of sand,
Lonely from the beginning of time until now!
Trees fall, the grass goes yellow with autumn.
I climb the towers and towers
        to watch out the barbarous land:
Desolate castle, the sky, the wide desert.
There is no wall left to this village.
Bones white with a thousand frosts,
High heaps, covered with trees and grass;
Who brought this to pass?
Who has brought the flaming imperial anger?
Who has brought the army with drums and with
        kettle-drums?
Barbarous kings.
A gracious spring, turned to blood-ravenous autumn,
A turmoil of wars-men, spread over the middle kingdom,
Three hundred and sixty thousand,
And sorrow, sorrow like rain.
Sorrow to go, and sorrow, sorrow returning.
Desolate, desolate fields,
And no children of warfare upon them,
        No longer the men for offence and defence.
Ah, how shall you know the dreary sorrow at the North Gate,
With Rihaku's name forgotten,
And we guardsmen fed to the tigers.

RIHAKU (LI PO)   49
TRANSLATED BY EZRA POUND

LAMENT OF A SOLDIER'S WIFE

My husband never desired the official seal of a marquis,
But a tiger's tally sent him to join the ranks in a foreign
　　land.
For many nights I was visited in my bedroom by bad
　　dreams,
Now I hear from the general's headquarters of the
　　army's defeat.
His body perished, yet his faded soldier's cloak remains;
His old comrade-in-arms has brought it home for me.
A woman, I'd never find the road to the border –
How could I get to far Wu-wei to find his unburied
　　bones?
I can only cut out paper pennants to summon back
　　his soul;
And turn them toward that place where we once parted.

　　TRANSLATED BY IRVING Y. LO

A FACE-OFF IN THE CRUSADES
from Jerusalem Delivered

It was a great, a strange, and wond'rous sight,
    When front to front those noble armies met,
How every troop, how in each troop each knight
    Stood prest to move, to fight, and praise to get.
Loose in the wind waved their ensigns light,
    Trembled the plumes that on their crests were set;
Their arms, impresses, colors, gold, and stone,
'Gainst the sun-beams smil'd, flamed, sparkled, shone:

Of dry-top'd oaks they seem'd two forests thick,
    So did each host with spears and pikes abound:
Bent were their bows, in rest their lances stick,
    Their hands shook swords, their slings held
        cobles round.
Each steed to run was ready, prest, and quick
    At his commander's spur, his hand, his sound;
He chafes, he stamps, careers, and turns about;
He foams, snorts, neighs, and fire and smoke
        breathes out.

Horror itself in that fair sight seem'd fair,
    And pleasure flew amid sad dread and fear;
The trumpets shrill that thunder'd in the air
    Were music mild and sweet to every ear;

The faithful camp, though less, yet seem'd more rare
    In that strange noise, more warlike, shrill, and clear,
In notes more sweet; the pagan trumpets jar:
These sung, their armors shin'd; those glister'd far.

The Christian trumpets give the deadly call,
    The Pagans' answer, and the fight accept.
The godly Frenchmen on their knees down fall
    To pray, and kiss'd the earth, and then up-leapt
To fight: the land between was vanish'd all;
    In combat close each host to other stepped;
For now the wings had skirmish hot begun,
And with their battles forth the footmen run.

BRITOMART KILLS THE AMAZON
from The Faerie Queene

But ere they reared hand, the Amazone
    Began the streight conditions to propound,
    With which she vsed still to tye her fone;
    To serue her so, as she the rest had bound.
    Which when the other heard, she sternly frownd
    For high disdaine of such indignity,
    And would no lenger treat, but bad them sound.
    For her no other termes should euer tie
Then what prescribed were by lawes of cheualrie.

The Trumpets sound, and they together run
    With greedy rage, and with their faulchins smot;
    Ne either sought the others strokes to shun,
    But through great fury both their skill forgot,
    And practicke vse in armes: ne spared not
    Their dainty parts, which nature had created
    So faire and tender, without staine or spot,
    For other vses, then they them translated;
Which they now hackt & hewd, as if such vse they
      hated,

As when a Tygre and a Lionesse
    Are met at spoyling of some hungry pray,
    Both challenge it with equall greedinesse:

But first the Tygre clawes thereon did lay;
    And therefore loth to loose her right away,
    Doth in defence thereof full stoutly stond:
    To which the Lion strongly doth gainesay,
    That she to hunt the beast first tooke in hond;
And therefore ought it haue, where euer she it fond.

Full fiercely layde the Amazon about,
    And dealt her blowes vnmercifully sore:
    Which *Britomart* withstood with courage stout,
    And them repaide againe with double more.
    So long they fought, that all the grassie flore
    Was fild with bloud, which from their sides did flow,
    And gushed through their armes, that all in gore
    They trode, and on the ground their liues did strow,
Like fruitles seede, of which vntimely death should
      grow.

At last proud *Radigund* with fell despight,
    Hauing by chaunce espide aduantage neare,
    Let driue at her with all her dreadfull might,
    And thus vpbrayding said; This token beare
    Vnto the man, whom thou doest loue so deare;
    And tell him for his sake thy life thou gauest.
    Which spitefull words she sore engrieu'd to heare,
    Thus answer'd; Lewdly thou my loue deprauest,
Who shortly must repent that now so vainely brauest.

Nath'lesse that stroke so cruell passage found,
    That glauncing on her shoulder plate, it bit
    Vnto the bone, and made a griesly wound,
    That she her shield through raging smart of it
    Could scarse vphold; yet soone she it requit.
    For hauing force increast through furious paine,
    She her so rudely on the helmet smit,
    That it empierced to the very braine,
And her proud person low prostrated on the plaine.

CAROL FOR THE VICTORY AT AGINCOURT

Deo gracias Anglia
Redde pro victoria

Our king went forth to Normandy
With grace and might of chivalry;
There God for him wrought marvelously:
Wherefore England may call and cry:
  "Deo gracias".

He set a stage, the sooth for to say,
To Harfleur town with royal array;
That town he won and made affray [attack]
That France shal rue till Doomèsday.
  "Deo gracias".

Then went our king with all his host
Through France, for all the French could boast
He spared, no dread, nor least nor most,
Till he came to Agincourt coast.
  "Deo gracias".

Then forsooth, that knight comèly
In Aginscourt field fought manly;
Through grace of God most mighty
He had both the field and the victory.
     "Deo gracias".

There dukes and earls, lord and baròn
Were taken and slain, and that well done,
And some were led into Londòn
With joy and mirth and great renown.
     "Deo gracias".

Now gracious God he saved our king,
His people and all his well-willing:
Give him good life, and good ending
That we with mirth may safely sing
     "Deo gracias".

KING HENRY EXHORTS HIS TROOPS
from Henry V, Act 3, scene i

    K. Hen.   Once more unto the breach, dear friends,
      once more;
Or close the wall up with our English dead.
In peace there's nothing so becomes a man
As modest stillness and humility;
But when the blast of war blows in our ears,
Then imitate the action of the tiger;
Stiffen the sinews, [conjure] up the blood,
Disguise fair nature with hard-favour'd rage;
Then lend the eye a terrible aspect;
Let it pry through the portage of the head
Like the brass cannon; let the brow o'erwhelm it
As fearfully as doth a galled rock
O'erhang and jutty his confounded base.
Swill'd with the wild and wasteful ocean.
Now set the teeth and stretch the nostril wide,
Hold hard the breath, and bend up every spirit
To his full height. On, on, you [noblest] English,
Whose blood is fet from fathers of war-proof!
Fathers that, like so many Alexanders,
Have in these parts from morn till even fought,
And sheath'd their swords for lack of argument.
Dishonour not your mothers; now attest
That those whom you call'd fathers did beget you.

Be copy now to [men] of grosser blood,
And teach them how to war. And you, good yeomen,
Whose limbs were made in England, show us here
The mettle of your pasture; let us swear
That you are worth your breeding, which I doubt not;
For there is none of you so mean and base
That hath not noble lustre in your eyes.
I see you stand like greyhounds in the slips,
[Straining] upon the start. The game's afoot!
Follow your spirit; and upon this charge
Cry, "God for Harry, England, and Saint George!"

WILLIAM SHAKESPEARE   59

BEFORE THE BATTLE OF AGINCOURT
from Henry V, Act 4, Prologue

Now entertain conjecture of a time
When creeping murmur and the poring dark
Fills the wide vessel of the universe.
From camp to camp, through the foul womb of night,
The hum of either army stilly sounds,
That the fix'd sentinels almost receive
The secret whispers of each other's watch.
Fire answers fire, and through their paly flames
Each battle sees the other's umber'd face.
Steed threatens steed, in high and boastful neighs
Piercing the night's dull ear; and from the tents
The armourers, accomplishing the knights,
With busy hammers closing rivets up,
Give dreadful note of preparation.
The country cocks do crow, the clocks do toll,
And the third hour of drowsy morning [name].
Proud of their numbers and secure in soul,
The confident and overlusty French
Do the low-rated English play at dice;
And chide the cripple tardy-gaited night,
Who like a foul and ugly witch doth limp
So tediously away. The poor condemned English,
Like sacrifices, by their watchful fires

Sit patiently and inly ruminate
The morning's danger; and their gesture sad,
Investing lank-lean cheeks and war-worn coats,
Presented them unto the gazing moon
So many horrid ghosts. O now, who will behold
The royal captain of this ruin'd band
Walking from watch to watch, from tent to tent,
Let him cry, "Praise and glory on his head!"
For forth he goes, and visits all his host,
Bids them good morrow with a modest smile,
And calls them brothers, friends, and countrymen.
Upon his royal face there is no note
How dread an army hath enrounded him;
Nor doth he dedicate one jot of colour
Unto the weary and all-watched night;
But freshly looks, and overbears attaint
With cheerful semblance and sweet majesty;
That every wretch, pining and pale before,
Beholding him, plucks comfort from his looks.
A largess universal, like the sun,
His liberal eye doth give to every one,
Thawing cold fear, that mean and gentle all
Behold, as may unworthiness define,
A little touch of Harry in the night.
And so our scene must to the battle fly;

Where – O for pity! – we shall much disgrace
With four or five most vile and ragged foils
(Right ill dispos'd, in brawl ridiculous)
The name of Agincourt. Yet sit and see,
Minding true things by what their mock'ries be.

FAREWELL TO ARMS
To Queen Elizabeth

His golden locks time hath to silver turned;
    O time too swift, O swiftness never ceasing!
His youth 'gainst time and age hath ever spurned,
    But spurned in vain; youth waneth by increasing:
Beauty, strength, youth, are flowers but fading seen;
Duty, faith, love, are roots, and ever green.

His helmet now shall make a hive for bees;
    And, lovers' sonnets turned to holy psalms,
A man-at-arms must now serve on his knees,
    And feed on prayers, which are age's alms:
But though from court to cottage he depart,
His saint is sure of his unspotted heart.

And when he saddest sits in homely cell,
    He'll teach his swains this carol for a song:
"Blest be the hearts that wish my sovereign well,
    Curst be the souls that think her any wrong."
Goddess, allow this agèd man his right,
To be your beadsman now, that was your knight.

SIR HENRY LEE

THE GLORIES OF OUR BLOOD
AND STATE

The glories of our blood and state
    Are shadows, not substantial things;
There is no armour against fate;
    Death lays his icy hand on kings:
        Sceptre and Crown
        Must tumble down,
And in the dust be equal made
With the poor crooked scythe and spade.

Some men with swords may reap the field,
    And plant fresh laurels where they kill:
But their strong nerves at last must yield;
    They tame but one another still:
        Early or late
        They stoop to fate,
And must give up their murmuring breath
When they, pale captives, creep to death.

The garlands wither on your brow;
    Then boast no more your mighty deeds;
Upon Death's purple altar now
    See where the victor-victim bleeds:

Your heads must come
To the cold tomb;
Only the actions of the just
Smell sweet, and blossom in their dust.

TO LUCASTA, GOING TO THE WARS

Tell me not, sweet, I am unkind,
    That from the nunnery
Of thy chaste breast and quiet mind
    To war and arms I fly.

True, a new mistress now I chase,
    The first foe in the field;
And with a stronger faith embrace
    A sword, a horse, a shield.

Yet this inconstancy is such
    As you too shall adore;
I could not love thee, dear, so much,
    Loved I not honour more.

GATHERING SONG OF
DONALD THE BLACK

Pibroch of Donuil Dhu,
   Pibroch of Donuil,
Wake thy wild voice anew,
   Summon Clan Conuil.
Come away, come away,
   Hark to the summons!
Come in your war-array,
   Gentles and commons.

Come from deep glen, and
   From mountain so rocky;
The war-pipe and pennon
   Are at Inverlocky.
Come every hill-plaid, and
   True heart that wears one,
Come every steel blade, and
   Strong hand that bears one.

Leave untended the herd,
   The flock without shelter;
Leave the corpse uninterr'd,
   The bride at the altar;
Leave the deer, leave the steer,
   Leave nets and barges:

Come with your fighting gear,
    Broadswords and targes.

Come as the winds come, when
    Forests are rended;
Come as the waves come, when
    Navies are stranded:
Faster come, faster come,
    Faster and faster,
Chief, vassal, page and groom,
    Tenant and master.

Fast they come, fast they come;
    See how they gather!
Wide waves the eagle plume,
    Blended with heather.
Cast your plaids, draw your blades,
    Forward each man set!
Pibroch of Donuil Dhu
    Knell for the onset!

THE BATTLE OF FLODDEN FIELD
from Marmion

Next morn the Baron climb'd the tower,
To view afar the Scottish power,
   Encamp'd on Flodden edge:
The white pavilions made a show,
Like remnants of the winter snow,
   Along the dusky ridge.
Long Marmion look'd: at length his eye
Unusual movement might descry
   Amid the shifting lines:
The Scottish host drawn out appears,
For, flashing on the hedge of spears
   The eastern sunbeam shines.
Their front now deepening, now extending;
Their flank inclining, wheeling, bending,
Now drawing back, and now descending,
The skilful Marmion well could know
They watch'd the motions of some foe,
Who travers'd on the plain below.

Even so it was. From Flodden ridge
   The Scots beheld the English host
   Leave Barmore-wood, their evening post,
   And heedful watch'd them as they cross'd
The Till by Twisel Bridge.

High sight it is, and haughty, while
    They dive into the deep defile;
    Beneath the cavern'd cliff they fall,
    Beneath the castle's airy wall;
By rock, by oak, by hawthorn-tree,
    Troop after troop are disappearing;
    Troop after troop their banners rearing,
Upon the eastern bank you see;
Still pouring down the rocky den,
    Where flows the sullen Till,
And rising from the dim-wood glen,
Standards on standards, men on men,
    In slow succession still,
And, sweeping o'er the Gothic arch,
And pressing on, in ceaseless march,
    To gain the opposing hill.
That morn, to many a trumpet clang,
Twisel! thy rock's deep echo rang;
And many a chief of birth and rank,
Saint Helen! at thy fountain drank.
Thy hawthorn glade, which now we see
In spring-tide bloom so lavishly,
Had then from many an axe its doom,
To give the marching columns room.

And why stands Scotland idly now,
Dark Flodden! on thy airy brow,

Since England gains the pass the while,
And struggles through the deep defile?
What checks the fiery soul of James?
Why sits that champion of the dames
    Inactive on his steed,
And sees, between him and his land,
Between him and Tweed's southern strand,
    His host Lord Surrey lead?
What 'vails the vain knight-errant's brand?
O, Douglas, for thy leading wand!
    Fierce Randolph, for thy speed!
O for one hour of Wallace wight,
Or well-skill'd Bruce, to rule the fight,
And cry "Saint Andrew and our right!"
Another sight had seen that morn,
From Fate's dark book a leaf been torn,
And Flodden had been Bannockbourne!
The precious hour has pass'd in vain,
And England's host has gain'd the plain;
Wheeling their march, and circling still,
Around the base of Flodden hill.

O FLODDEN FIELD

The learned King fought
like a fool, flanked
and outtricked, who hacked
in a corner of cousins
until the ten thousand
swords lay broken,
and the women walked
in their houses alone.

On a journey among horses,
the spirit of a man who died
only a week ago
is walking through heather
and forgets that its body
had seventy years.
Wild horses are singing,
and voices of the rocks.

The spirit from the boneyard
finds a new life, in the field
where the King's wound
built the blackness of Glasgow
and the smoke of the air.
The spirit, like a boy,
picks up from the heather
a whole sword.

THE WAR SONG OF DINAS VAWR

The mountain sheep are sweeter,
    But the valley sheep are fatter;
We therefore deemed it meeter
    To carry off the latter.
We made an expedition;
    We met a host, and quelled it;
We forced a strong position,
    And killed the men who held it.

On Dyfed's richest valley,
    Where herds of kine were browsing,
We made a mighty sally
    To furnish our carousing.
Fierce warriors rushed to meet us;
    We met them, and o'erthrew them:
They struggled hard to beat us;
    But we conquered them, and slew them.

As we drove our prize at leisure,
    The king marched forth to catch us:
His rage surpassed all measure,
    But his people could not match us.
He fled to his hall-pillars;
    And, ere our force we led off,
Some sacked his house and cellars,
    While others cut his head off.

We there, in strife bewildering,
    Spilt blood enough to swim in:
We orphaned many children,
    And widowed many women.
The eagles and the ravens
    We glutted with our foemen;
The heroes and the cravens,
    The spearmen and the bowmen.

We brought away from battle,
    And much their land bemoaned them,
Two thousand head of cattle,
    And the head of him who owned them:
Ednyfed, King of Dyfed,
    His head was borne before us;
His wine and beasts supplied our feasts,
    And his overthrow, our chorus.

BEFORE AND AFTER NAPOLEON

TO THE DUKE OF MARLBOROUGH
from The Campaign

But, O my muse, what numbers wilt thou find
To sing the furious troops in battle joined!
Methinks I hear the drum's tumultuous sound
The victor's shouts and dying groans confound,
The dreadful burst of cannon rend the skies,
And all the thunder of the battle rise.
'Twas then great Marlborough's mighty soul
    was proved
That, in the shock of charging hosts unmoved,
Amidst confusion, horror, and despair,
Examined all the dreadful scenes of war;
In peaceful thought the field of death surveyed,
To fainting squadrons sent the timely aid,
Inspired repulsed battalions to engage,
And taught the doubtful battle where to rage.
So when an angel by divine command
With rising tempests shakes a guilty land,
Such as of late o'er pale Britannia past,
Calm and serene he drives the furious blast;
And, pleased the Almighty's orders to perform,
Rides in the whirlwind, and directs the storm.

AFTER BLENHEIM

It was a summer evening,
   Old Kaspar's work was done,
And he before his cottage door
   Was sitting in the sun,
And by him sported on the green
His little grandchild Wilhelmine.

She saw her brother Peterkin
   Roll something large and round,
Which he beside the rivulet
   In playing there had found;
He came to ask what he had found,
That was so large, and smooth, and round.

Old Kaspar took it from the boy,
   Who stood expectant by;
And then the old man shook his head,
   And, with a natural sigh,
"'Tis some poor fellow's skull," said he,
"Who fell in the great victory.

"I find them in the garden,
   For there's many here about;
And often when I go to plough,
   The ploughshare turns them out!

For many thousand men," said he,
"Were slain in that great victory."

"Now tell us what 'twas all about,"
    Young Peterkin, he cries;
And little Wilhelmine looks up
    With wonder-waiting eyes;
"Now tell us all about the war,
And what they fought each other for."

"It was the English," Kaspar cried,
    "Who put the French to rout;
But what they fought each other for,
    I could not well make out;
But everybody said," quoth he,
"That 'twas a famous victory.

"My father lived at Blenheim then,
    Yon little stream hard by;
They burnt his dwelling to the ground,
    And he was forced to fly;
So with his wife and child he fled,
Nor had he where to rest his head.

"With fire and sword the country round
    Was wasted far and wide,
And many a childing mother then,

And new-born baby died;
But things like that, you know, must be
At every famous victory.

"They say it was a shocking sight
    After the field was won;
For many thousand bodies here
    Lay rotting in the sun;
But things like that, you know, must be
After a famous victory.

"Great praise the Duke of Marlbro' won,
    And our good Prince Eugene."
"Why 'twas a very wicked thing!"
    Said little Wilhelmine.
"Nay . . . nay . . . my little girl," quoth he,
"It was a famous victory.

"And everybody praised the Duke
    Who this great fight did win."
"But what good came of it at last?"
    Quoth little Peterkin.
"Why that I cannot tell," said he,
"But 'twas a famous victory."

THE DRUM

I hate that drum's discordant sound,
Parading round, and round, and round:
To thoughtless youth it pleasure yields,
And lures from cities and from fields,
To sell their liberty for charms
Of tawdry lace, and glittering arms;
And when Ambition's voice commands,
To march, and fight, and fall, in foreign lands.

I hate that drum's discordant sound,
Parading round, and round, and round:
To me it talks of ravaged plains,
And burning towns, and ruined swains,
And mangled limbs, and dying groans,
And widows' tears, and orphans' moans;
And all that Misery's hand bestows,
To fill the catalogue of human woes.

CONCORD HYMN

Sung at the completion of the Battle Monument,
19 April 1836

By the rude bridge that arched the flood,
　　Their flag to April's breeze unfurled,
Here once the embattled farmers stood,
　　And fired the shot heard round the world.

The foe long since in silence slept;
　　Alike the conqueror silent sleeps;
And Time the ruined bridge has swept
　　Down the dark stream which seaward creeps.

On this green bank, by this soft stream,
　　We set today a votive stone;
That memory may their deed redeem,
　　When, like our sires, our sons are gone.

Spirit, that made those heroes dare
　　To die, and leave their children free,
Bid Time and Nature gently spare
　　The shaft we raise to them and thee.

AFTER THE AMERICAN REBELLION

The snow lies thick on Valley Forge,
    The ice on the Delaware,
But the poor dead soldiers of King George
    They neither know nor care.

Not though the earliest primrose break
    On the sunny side of the lane,
And scuffling rookeries awake
    Their England's spring again.

They will not stir when the drifts are gone,
    Or the ice melts out of the bay:
And the men that served with Washington
    Lie all as still as they.

They will not stir though the mayflower blows
    In the moist dark woods of pine,
And every rock-strewn pasture shows
    Mullein and columbine.

Each for his land, in a fair fight,
    Encountered, strove, and died,
And the kindly earth that knows no spite
    Covers them side by side.

She is too busy to think of war;
    She has all the world to make gay;
And, behold, the yearly flowers are
    Where they were in our fathers' day!

Golden-rod by the pasture wall
    When the columbine is dead,
And sumach leaves that turn, in fall,
    Bright as the blood they shed.

HOHENLINDEN

On Linden, when the sun was low,
All bloodless lay the untrodden snow,
And dark as winter was the flow
    Of Iser, rolling rapidly.

But Linden saw another sight,
When the drum beat, at dead of night,
Commanding fires of death to light
    The darkness of her scenery.

By torch and trumpet fast arrayed,
Each horseman drew his battle blade,
And furious every charger neighed
    To join the dreadful revelry.

Then shook the hills, with thunder riven;
Then rushed the steed, to battle driven;
And, louder than the bolts of heaven,
    Far flashed the red artillery.

But redder yet that light shall glow,
On Linden's hills of stainèd snow;
And bloodier yet, the torrent flow
    Of Iser, rolling rapidly.

'Tis morn; but scarce yon level sun
Can pierce the war-clouds, rolling dun,
Where furious Frank, and fiery Hun,
    Shout in their sulphurous canopy.

The combat deepens. On, ye brave,
Who rush to glory, or the grave!
Wave, Munich, all thy banners wave,
    And charge with all thy chivalry!

Few, few shall part, where many meet!
The snow shall be their winding sheet,
And every turf, beneath their feet,
    Shall be a soldier's sepulchre.

INCIDENT OF THE FRENCH CAMP

You know, we French stormed Ratisbon:
    A mile or so away,
On a little mound, Napoleon
    Stood on our storming-day;
With neck out-thrust, you fancy how,
    Legs wide, arms locked behind,
As if to balance the prone brow
    Oppressive with its mind.

Just as perhaps he mused "My plans
    That soar, to earth may fall,
Let once my army-leader Lannes
    Waver at yonder wall," –
Out 'twixt the battery-smokes there flew
    A rider, bound on bound
Full-galloping; nor bridle drew
    Until he reached the mound.

Then off there flung in smiling joy,
    And held himself erect
By just his horse's mane, a boy:
    You hardly could suspect –
(So tight he kept his lips compressed,
    Scarce any blood came through)
You looked twice ere you saw his breast
    Was all but shot in two.

"Well," cried he, "Emperor, by God's grace
    We've got you Ratisbon!
The Marshal's in the market-place,
    And you'll be there anon
To see your flag-bird flap his vans
    Where I, to heart's desire,
Perched him!" The chief's eye flashed; his plans
    Soared up again like fire.

The chief's eye flashed; but presently
    Softened itself, as sheathes
A film the mother-eagle's eye
    When her bruised eaglet breathes;
"You're wounded!" "Nay," the soldier's pride
    Touched to the quick, he said:
"I'm killed, Sire!" And his chief beside,
    Smiling the boy fell dead.

ON WAR *from* Don Juan

Oh, thou eternal Homer! who couldst charm
    All ears, though long; all ages, though so short,
By merely wielding with poetic arm
    Arms to which men will never more resort,
Unless gunpowder should be found to harm
    Much less than is the hope of every court,
Which now is leagued young Freedom to annoy;
But they will not find Liberty a Troy: —

Oh, thou eternal Homer! I have now
    To paint a siege, wherein more men were slain,
With deadlier engines and a speedier blow,
    Than in thy Greek gazette of that campaign;
And yet, like all men else, I must allow,
    To vie with thee would be about as vain
As for a brook to cope with ocean's flood;
But still we moderns equal you in blood;

If not in poetry, at least in fact;
    And fact is truth, the grand desideratum!
Of which, howe'er the Muse describes each act,
    There should be ne'ertheless a slight substratum.
But now the town is going to be attacked;
    Great deeds are doing — how shall I relate 'em?
Souls of immortal generals! Phœbus watches
To colour up his rays from your despatches.

Oh, ye great bulletins of Bonaparte!
   Oh, ye less grand long lists of killed and wounded!
Shade of Leonidas, who fought so hearty,
   When my poor Greece was once, as now,
      surrounded!
Oh, Cæsar's Commentaries! now impart, ye
   Shadows of glory! (lest I be confounded)
A portion of your fading twilight hues,
So beautiful, so fleeting, to the Muse.

When I call "fading" martial immortality,
   I mean, that every age and every year,
And almost every day, in sad reality,
   Some sucking hero is compelled to rear,
Who, when we come to sum up the totality
   Of deeds to human happiness most dear,
Turns out to be a butcher in great business,
Afflicting young folks with a sort of dizziness.

Medals, rank, ribands, lace, embroidery, scarlet,
   Are things immortal to immortal man,
As purple to the Babylonian harlot:
   An uniform to boys is like a fan
To women; there is scarce a crimson varlet
   But deems himself the first in Glory's van.
But Glory's glory; and if you would find
What that is — ask the pig who sees the wind!

At least *he feels it*, and some say he *sees*,
    Because he runs before it like a pig;
Or, if that simple sentence should displease,
    Say, that he scuds before it like a brig,
A schooner, or – but it is time to ease
    This Canto, ere my Muse perceives fatigue.
The next shall ring a peal to shake all people,
Like a bob-major from a village steeple.

Hark! through the silence of the cold, dull night,
    The hum of armies gathering rank on rank!
Lo! dusky masses steal in dubious sight
    Along the leaguered wall and bristling bank
Of the armed river, while with straggling light
    The stars peep through the vapours dim and dank,
Which curl in curious wreaths: – how soon the smoke
Of Hell shall pall them in a deeper cloak!

Here pause we for the present – as even then
    That awful pause, dividing life from death,
Struck for an instant on the hearts of men,
    Thousands of whom were drawing their last breath!
A moment – and all will be life again!
    The march! the charge! the shouts of either faith!
Hurra! and Allah! and – one moment more,
The death-cry drowning in the battle's roar.

BATTLE OF THE BALTIC

    Of Nelson and the North
Sing the glorious day's renown,
    When to battle fierce came forth
All the might of Denmark's crown,
And her arms along the deep proudly shone;
    By each gun the lighted brand
    In a bold, determined hand,
    And the Prince of all the land
      Led them on.

    Like leviathans afloat
Lay their bulwarks on the brine;
    While the sign of battle flew
On the lofty British line:
It was ten of April morn by the chime:
    As they drifted on their path
    There was silence deep as death;
    And the boldest held his breath
      For a time.

    But the might of England flush'd
To anticipate the scene;
    And her van the fleeter rush'd
O'er the deadly space between.
"Hearts of oak!" our captains cried, when each gun

From its adamantine lips
Spread a death-shade round the ships,
Like the hurricane eclipse
    Of the sun.

    Again! again! again!
And the havoc did not slack,
    Till a feeble cheer the Dane
To our cheering sent us back;
Their shots along the deep slowly boom:
    Then ceased – and all is wail,
    As they strike the shatter'd sail;
    Or in conflagration pale
        Light the gloom.

    Out spoke the victor then
As he hail'd them o'er the wave,
    "Ye are brothers! ye are men!
And we conquer but to save:
So peace instead of death let us bring:
    But yield, proud foe, thy fleet
    With the crews, at England's feet,
    And make submission meet
        To our King."

    Then Denmark blest our chief
That he gave her wounds repose;

And the sounds of joy and grief
From her people wildly rose,
As death withdrew his shades from the day:
While the sun look'd smiling bright
O'er a wide and woeful sight,
Where the fires of funeral light
Died away.

Now joy, old England, raise
For the tidings of thy might,
By the festal cities' blaze,
Whilst the wine cup shines in light;
And yet amidst that joy and uproar,
Let us think of them that sleep
Full many a fathom deep
By thy wild and stormy steep,
Elsinore!

Brave hearts! to Britain's pride
Once so faithful and so true,
On the deck of fame that died
With the gallant good Riou:
Soft sigh the winds of heaven o'er their grave!
While the billow mournful rolls
And the mermaid's song condoles,
Singing glory to the souls
Of the brave!

94   THOMAS CAMPBELL

THE YEAR 1812

Year well remembered! Happy who beheld thee!
The commons knew thee as the year of yield,
But as the year of war, the soldiery.

Rumours and skyward prodigies revealed
The poet's dream, the tale on old men's lips,
The spring when kine preferred the barren field.

Short of the acres green with growing tips
They halted lowing, chewed the winter's cud;
The men awaited an apocalypse.

Languid the farmer sought his livelihood
And checked his team and gazed, as if enquiring
What marvels gathered westward while he stood.

He asked the stork, whose white returning wing
Already spread above its native pine
Had raised the early standard of the Spring.

From swallows gathering frozen mud to line
Their tiny homes, or in loud regiments
Ranged over water, he implored a sign.

The thickets hear each night as dusk descends

The woodcock's call. The forests hear the geese
Honk, and go down. The crane's voice never ends.

What storms have whirled them from what shaken
        seas,
The watchers ask, that they should come so soon?
Or in the feathered world, what mutinies?

For now fresh migrants of a brighter plume
Than finch or plover gleam above the hills,
Impend, descend, and on our meadows loom.

Cavalry! Troop after troop it spills
With strange insignia, strangely armed,
As snow in a spring thaw fills

The valley roads. From the forests long
Bright bayonets issue, as brigades of foot
Debouch like ants, form up, and densely throng;

All heading north as if the bird, the scout,
Had led men here from halcyon lands, impelled
By instincts too imperative to doubt.

War! the war! – a meaning that transpires
To the remotest corner. In the wood
Beyond whose bounds no rustic mind enquires,

Where in the sky the peasant understood
Only the wind's cry, and on earth the brute's
(And all his visitors the neighbourhood),

A sudden glare! A crash! A ball that shoots
Far from the field, makes its impeded way,
Rips through the branches and lays bare the roots.

The bearded bison trembles, and at bay
Heaves to his forelegs, ruffs his mane, and glares
At sudden sparks that glitter on the spray.

The stray bomb spins and hisses; as he stares,
Bursts. And the beast that never knew alarm
Blunders in panic to profounder lairs.

"Whither the battle?" – and the young men arm.
The women pray, "God is Napoleon's shield,
Napoleon ours", as to the outcome calm.

Spring well remembered! Happy who saw thee then,
Spring of the war, Spring of the mighty yield,
That promised corn but ripened into men.

ADAM MICKIEWICZ   97
TRANSLATED BY DONALD DAVIE

YE MARINERS OF ENGLAND

Ye Mariners of England
    That guard our native seas!
Whose flag has braved a thousand years
    The battle and the breeze!
Your glorious standard launch again
    To match another foe;
And sweep through the deep,
    While the stormy winds do blow!
While the battle rages loud and long
    And the stormy winds do blow.

The spirits of your fathers
    Shall start from every wave –
For the deck it was their field of fame,
    And Ocean was their grave:
Where Blake and mighty Nelson fell
    Your manly hearts shall glow,
As ye sweep through the deep,
    While the stormy winds do blow!
While the battle rages loud and long
    And the stormy winds do blow.

Britannia needs no bulwarks,
    No towers along the steep;
Her march is o'er the mountain-waves,
    Her home is on the deep.

With thunders from her native oak
　　She quells the floods below,
As they roar on the shore,
　　When the stormy winds do blow!
When the battle rages loud and long,
　　And the stormy winds do blow.

The meteor flag of England
　　Shall yet terrific burn;
Till danger's troubled night depart
　　And the star of peace return.
Then, then, ye ocean-warriors!
　　Our song and feast shall flow
To the fame of your name,
　　When the storm has ceased to blow!
When the fiery fight is heard no more,
　　And the storm has ceased to blow.

THE GRENADIERS

To France were returning two grenadiers
From Russia where they had been taken.
And when they came to the German frontiers,
They hung down their heads forsaken.

There sadly they heard the people tell
How France had been shattered and shaken,
Her Grand Army smashed by shot and shell,
And the Emperor, the Emperor was taken.

Together they wept, the grenadiers,
The sorrowful story learning.
Said one: "Ah woe!" with trembling tears,
"Woe's me, how my old wound is burning."

The other said: "The play is done –
Cold death I'd gladly cherish;
But ah, I have a wife and son,
Without me they would perish."

"Who cares for child? who cares for wife?
In my breast deeper longings awaken;
Let them all go begging to save their life –
The Emperor, the Emperor is taken!

"O grant me, comrade, one request:
When I am dead, if you love me,
O take my corpse to France, to rest
With the soil of France above me.

"The Cross of Honor with crimson band
Lay on my breast to pride me,
Give me my musket in my hand,
And gird my sword beside me.

"Thus will I listen and lie evermore
In my grave like a sentry staying,
Till one day I hear the cannon's roar
And horses trampling and neighing.

"That day will my Emperor ride over my grave,
Bright swords and lances attending,
That day will I rise fully armed from the grave,
The Emperor, the Emperor defending!"

HEINRICH HEINE   101
TRANSLATED BY HAL DRAPER

DEFENCE OF FORT McHENRY

O! say can you see, by the dawn's early light,
    What so proudly we hail'd at the twilight's last
        gleaming,
Whose broad stripes and bright stars through the perilous
        fight,
    O'er the ramparts we watch'd, were so gallantly
        streaming?
      And the rockets' red glare, the bombs bursting in air,
      Gave proof through the night that our flag was still
        there –
        O! say, does that star-spangled banner yet wave
        O'er the land of the free, and the home of the brave.

On the shore, dimly seen through the mists of the deep,
    Where the foe's haughty host in dread silence reposes,
What is that which the breeze o'er the towering steep,
    As it fitfully blows, half conceals, half discloses?
      Now it catches the gleam of the morning's first beam,
      In full glory reflected now shines on the stream –
        'Tis the star-spangled banner, O! long may it wave
        O'er the land of the free, and the home of the brave.

And where is that band who so vauntingly swore
    That the havock of war and the battle's confusion
A home and a country should leave us no more?

Their blood has wash'd out their foul foot-steps'
        pollution.
    No refuge could save the hireling and slave,
    From the terror of flight or the gloom of the grave;
        And the star-spangled banner in triumph doth wave
        O'er the land of the free, and the home of the brave.

O! thus be it ever when freemen shall stand
    Between their lov'd home, and the war's desolation,
Blest with vict'ry and peace, may the heav'n-rescued land
    Praise the power that hath made and preserv'd us a
        nation!
        Then conquer we must, when our cause it is just,
        And this be our motto – "In God is our trust!"
            And the star-spangled banner in triumph shall wave
            O'er the land of the free, and the home of the brave.

THE DREAM

Deep in a dale, immovable and choking,
I lay alone, my breast by bullets ripped;
At scorching noon my open wound was smoking,
And drop by drop my blood congealed and dripped.

The dale was empty after the invasion,
The mountains stood inhospitably steep,
Their summits cracked in midday heat Caucasian,
But I was cold in my unbroken sleep.

I slept and dreamed that women decked with roses
Had come together for a merry feast;
They drank and laughed and sat in languid poses.
They talked of me; their talking never ceased.

But 'mid the guests there was a silent maiden
Who did not laugh and did not talk or dance.
The table stood with rich refreshments laden,
But something plunged her feelings in a trance.

She dreamed of someone motionless and choking;
A man she knew was dying in a dale,
At scorching noon his open wound was smoking,
And all his blood became congealed and stale.

THE CHARGE OF THE
LIGHT BRIGADE

Half a league, half a league,
   Half a league onward,
All in the valley of Death
   Rode the six hundred.
"Forward, the Light Brigade!
Charge for the guns!" he said:
Into the valley of Death
   Rode the six hundred.

"Forward, the Light Brigade!"
Was there a man dismayed?
Not though the soldier knew
   Some one had blundered:
Their's not to make reply,
Their's not to reason why,
Their's but to do and die:
Into the valley of Death
   Rode the six hundred.

Cannon to right of them,
Cannon to left of them,
Cannon in front of them
   Volleyed and thundered;
Stormed at with shot and shell,

Boldly they rode and well,
Into the jaws of Death,
Into the mouth of Hell
   Rode the six hundred.

Flashed all their sabres bare,
Flashed as they turned in air
Sabring the gunners there,
Charging an army, while
   All the world wondered:
Plunged in the battery-smoke
Right through the line they broke;
Cossack and Russian
Reeled from the sabre-stroke
   Shattered and sundered.
Then they rode back, but not
   Not the six hundred.

Cannon to right of them,
Cannon to left of them,
Cannon behind them
   Volleyed and thundered;
Stormed at with shot and shell,
While horse and hero fell,
They that had fought so well
Came through the jaws of Death,
Back from the mouth of Hell,

All that was left of them,
    Left of six hundred.

When can their glory fade?
O the wild charge they made!
    All the world wondered.
Honour the charge they made!
Honour the Light Brigade,
    Noble six hundred!

1887

From Clee to heaven the beacon burns,
　　The shires have seen it plain,
From north and south the sign returns
　　And beacons burn again.

Look left, look right, the hills are bright,
　　The dales are light between,
Because 'tis fifty years to-night
　　That God has saved the Queen.

Now, when the flame they watch not towers
　　About the soil they trod,
Lads, we'll remember friends of ours
　　Who shared the work with God.

To skies that knit their heartstrings right,
　　To fields that bred them brave,
The saviours come not home to-night:
　　Themselves they could not save.

It dawns in Asia, tombstones show
　　And Shropshire names are read;
And the Nile spills his overflow
　　Beside the Severn's dead.

We pledge in peace by farm and town
    The Queen they served in war,
And fire the beacons up and down
    The land they perished for.

"God save the Queen" we living sing,
    From height to height 'tis heard;
And with the rest your voices ring,
    Lads of the Fifty-third.

Oh, God will save her, fear you not:
    Be you the men you've been,
Get you the sons your fathers got,
    And God will save the Queen.

DANNY DEEVER

"What are the bugles blowin' for?" said Files-on-
    Parade.
"To turn you out, to turn you out," the Colour-
    Sergeant said.
"What makes you look so white, so white?" said
    Files-on-Parade.
"I'm dreadin' what I've got to watch," the Colour-
    Sergeant said.
For they're hangin' Danny Deever, you can hear
    the Dead March play,
The Regiment's in 'ollow square – they're hangin'
    him to-day;
They've taken of his buttons off an' cut his stripes
    away,
An' they're hangin' Danny Deever in the mornin'.

"What makes the rear-rank breathe so 'ard?" said
    Files-on-Parade.
"It's bitter cold, it's bitter cold," the Colour-
    Sergeant said.
"What makes that front-rank man fall down?"
    said Files-on-Parade.
"A touch o' sun, a touch o' sun," the Colour-
    Sergeant said.

They are hangin' Danny Deever, they are
　　marchin' of 'im round,
They 'ave 'alted Danny Deever by 'is coffin on the
　　ground;
An' 'e'll swing in 'arf a minute for a sneakin'
　　shootin' hound –
O they're hangin' Danny Deever in the mornin'!

"'Is cot was right-'and cot to mine," said Files-on-
　　Parade.
"'E's sleepin' out an' far to-night," the Colour-
　　Sergeant said.
"I've drunk 'is beer a score o' times," said Files-
　　on-Parade.
"'E's drinkin' bitter beer alone," the Colour-
　　Sergeant said.
They are hangin' Danny Deever, you must mark
　　'im to 'is place,
For 'e shot a comrade sleepin' – you must look 'im
　　in the face;
Nine 'undred of 'is county an' the Regiment's
　　disgrace,
While they're hangin' Danny Deever in the
　　mornin'.

"What's that so black agin the sun?" said Files-
　　on-Parade.

"It's Danny fightin' 'ard for life," the Colour-
    Sergeant said.
"What's that that whimpers over'ead?" said Files-
    on-Parade.
"It's Danny's soul that's passin' now," the Colour-
    Sergeant said.
For they've done with Danny Deever, you can 'ear
    the quickstep play,
The Regiment's in column, an' they're marchin'
    us away;
Ho! the young recruits are shakin', an' they'll
    want their beer to-day,
After hangin' Danny Deever in the mornin'!

ODE, INSCRIBED TO W. H. CHANNING

Though loath to grieve
The evil time's sole patriot,
I cannot leave
My honied thought
For the priest's cant,
Or statesman's rant.

If I refuse
My study for their politique,
Which at the best is trick,
The angry Muse
Puts confusion in my brain.

But who is he that prates
Of the culture of mankind,
Of better arts and life?
Go, blindworm, go,
Behold the famous States
Harrying Mexico
With rifle and with knife!

Or who, with accent bolder,
Dare praise the freedom-loving mountaineer?

I found by thee, O rushing Contoocook!
And in thy valleys, Agiochook!
The jackals of the negro-holder.

The God who made New Hampshire
Taunted the lofty land
With little men; —
Small bat and wren
House in the oak: —
If earth-fire cleave
The upheaved land, and bury the folk,
The southern crocodile would grieve.
Virtue palters; Right is hence;
Freedom praised, but hid;
Funeral eloquence
Rattles the coffin-lid.

What boots thy zeal,
O glowing friend,
That would indignant rend
The northland from the south?
Wherefore? to what good end?
Boston Bay and Bunker Hill
Would serve things still; —
Things are of the snake.

The horseman serves the horse,
The neatherd serves the neat,
The merchant serves the purse,
The eater serves his meat;
'Tis the day of the chattel,
Web to weave, and corn to grind;
Things are in the saddle,
And ride mankind.

There are two laws discrete,
Not reconciled, –
Law for man, and law for thing;
The last builds town and fleet,
But it runs wild,
And doth the man unking.

'Tis fit the forest fall,
The steep be graded,
The mountain tunnelled,
The sand shaded,
The orchard planted,
The glebe tilled,
The prairie granted,
The steamer built.

Let man serve law for man;
Live for friendship, live for love,

For truth's and harmony's behoof;
The state may follow how it can,
As Olympus follows Jove.

    Yet do not I implore
The wrinkled shopman to my sounding woods,
Nor bid the unwilling senator
Ask votes of thrushes in the solitudes.
Every one to his chosen work; —
Foolish hands may mix and mar;
Wise and sure the issues are.
Round they roll till dark is light,
Sex to sex, and even to odd; —
The over-god
Who marries Right to Might,
Who peoples, unpeoples, —
He who exterminates
Races by stronger races,
Black by white faces, —
Knows to bring honey
Out of the lion;
Grafts gentlest scion
On pirate and Turk.

The Cossack eats Poland,
Like stolen fruit;
Her last noble is ruined,

Her last poet mute:
Straight, into double band
The victors divide;
Half for freedom strike and stand; –
The astonished Muse finds thousands at her side.

THE AMERICAN
CIVIL WAR

THE PORTENT

Hanging from the beam,
    Slowly swaying (such the law),
Gaunt the shadow on your green,
    Shenandoah!
The cut is on the crown
(Lo, John Brown),
And the stabs shall heal no more.

Hidden in the cap
    Is the anguish none can draw;
So your future veils its face,
    Shenandoah!
But the streaming beard is shown
(Weird John Brown),
The meteor of the war.

THE ARSENAL AT SPRINGFIELD

This is the Arsenal. From floor to ceiling,
    Like a huge organ, rise the burnished arms;
But from their silent pipes no anthem pealing
    Startles the villages with strange alarms.

Ah! what a sound will rise, how wild and dreary,
    When the death-angel touches those swift keys!
What loud lament and dismal Miserere
    Will mingle with their awful symphonies!

I hear even now the infinite fierce chorus,
    The cries of agony, the endless groan,
Which, through the ages that have gone before us,
    In long reverberations reach our own.

On helm and harness rings the Saxon hammer,
    Through Cimbric forest roars the Norseman's song,
And loud, amid the universal clamour,
    O'er distant deserts sounds the Tartar gong.

I hear the Florentine, who from his palace
    Wheels out his battle-bell with dreadful din,
And Aztec priests upon their teocallis
    Beat the wild war-drums made of serpent's skin;

The tumult of each sacked and burning village;
    The shout that every prayer for mercy drowns;
The soldiers' revels in the midst of pillage;
    The wail of famine in beleaguered towns;

The bursting shell, the gateway wrenched asunder,
    The rattling musketry, the clashing blade;
And ever and anon, in tones of thunder,
    The diapason of the cannonade.

Is it, O man, with such discordant noises,
    With such accursed instruments as these,
Thou drownest Nature's sweet and kindly voices,
    And jarrest the celestial harmonies?

Were half the power that fills the world with terror,
    Were half the wealth bestowed on camps and courts,
Given to redeem the human mind from error,
    There were no need of arsenals or forts:

The warrior's name would be a name abhorrèd!
    And every nation that should lift again
Its hand against a brother, on its forehead
    Would wear for evermore the curse of Cain.

Down the dark future, through long generations,
    The echoing sounds grow fainter and then cease;

And like a bell, with solemn, sweet vibrations,
    I hear once more the voice of Christ say, "Peace!"

Peace! and no longer from its brazen portals
    The blast of War's great organ shakes the skies!
But beautiful as songs of the immortals,
    The holy melodies of love arise.

THE BATTLE HYMN OF THE REPUBLIC

Mine eyes have seen the glory of the coming of the
    Lord:
He is trampling out the vintage where the grapes of
    wrath are stored;
He hath loosed the fatal lightning of His terrible swift
    sword:
    His truth is marching on.

I have seen Him in the watch-fires of a hundred
    circling camps,
They have builded Him an altar in the evening dews
    and damps;
I can read His righteous sentence by the dim and
    flaring lamps:
    His day is marching on.

I have read a fiery gospel writ in burnished rows of
    steel:
"As ye deal with my contemners, so with you my grace
    shall deal;
Let the Hero, born of woman, crush the serpent with
    his heel,
    Since God is marching on."

He has sounded forth the trumpet that shall never call
    retreat;

He is sifting out the hearts of men before his judgment
    seat:
Oh, be swift, my soul, to answer Him! Be jubilant,
    my feet!
    Our God is marching on.

In the beauty of the lilies Christ was born across
    the sea,
With a glory in his bosom that transfigures you
    and me:
As he died to make men holy, let us die to make
    men free,
    While God is marching on.

A VISION OF THE CIVIL WAR

"I see the champion sword-strokes flash;
  I see them fall and hear them clash;
  I hear the murderous engines crash;
I see a brother stoop to loose a foeman-brother's
      bloody sash.

"I see the torn and mangled corse,
  The dead and dying heaped in scores,
  The headless rider by his horse,
The wounded captive bayoneted through and through
      without remorse.

"I hear the dying sufferer cry,
  With his crushed face turned to the sky,
  I see him crawl in agony
To the foul pool, and bow his head into its bloody slime
      and die.

"I see the assassin crouch and fire,
  I see his victim fall – expire;
  I see the murderer creeping nigher
To strip the dead: He turns the head: The face! The son
      beholds his sire!

"I hear the curses and the thanks;
  I see the mad charge on the flanks,

The rents – the gaps – the broken ranks, –
The vanquished squadrons driven headlong down
 the river's bridgeless banks.

"I see the death-gripe on the plain,
The grappling monsters on the main,
The tens of thousands that are slain,
And all the speechless suffering and agony of heart
 and brain.

"I see the dark and bloody spots,
The crowded rooms and crowded cots,
The bleaching bones, the battle-blots, –
And writ on many a nameless grave, a legend of
 forget-me-nots.

"I see the gorgéd prison-den,
The dead line and the pent-up pen,
The thousands quartered in the fen,
The living-deaths of skin and bone that were the
 goodly shapes of men.

"And still the bloody Dew must fall!
And His great Darkness with the Pall
Of His dread judgment cover all,
Till the Dead Nation rise Transformed by Truth to
 triumph over all!"

THE CONFLICT OF CONVICTIONS

On starry heights
    A bugle wails the long recall;
Derision stirs the deep abyss,
    Heaven's ominous silence over all.
Return, return, O eager Hope,
    And face man's latter fall.
Events, they make the dreamers quail;
Satan's old age is strong and hale,
A disciplined captain, gray in skill,
And Raphael a white enthusiast still;
Dashed aims, whereat Christ's martyrs pale,
Shall Mammon's slaves fulfill?

> (*Dismantle the fort,*
> *Cut down the fleet —*
> *Battle no more shall be!*
> *While the fields for fight in æons to come*
> *Congeal beneath the sea.*)

The terrors of truth and dart of death
    To faith alike are vain;
Though comets, gone a thousand years,
      Return again,
Patient she stands — she can no more —
And waits, nor heeds she waxes hoar.

> (*At a stony gate,*
> *A statue of stone,*
> *Weed overgrown —*
> *Long 'twill wait!*)

But God his former mind retains,
   Confirms his old decree;
The generations are inured to pains,
   And strong Necessity
Surges, and heaps Time's strand with wrecks.
   The People spread like a weedy grass,
   The thing they will they bring to pass,
And prosper to the apoplex.
The rout it herds around the heart,
   The ghost is yielded in the gloom;
Kings wag their heads — Now save thyself
   Who wouldst rebuild the world in bloom.

> (*Tide-mark*
> *And top of the ages' strife,*
> *Verge where they called the world to come,*
> *The last advance of life —*
> *Ha ha, the rust on the Iron Dome!*)

Nay, but revere the hid event;
   In the cloud a sword is girded on,

I mark a twinkling in the tent
    Of Michael the warrior one.
Senior wisdom suits not now,
The light is on the youthful brow.

> (*Ay, in caves the miner see:*
> *His forehead bears a taper dim;*
> *Darkness so he feebly braves*
> *Which foldeth him!*)

But He who rules is old – is old:
Ah! faith is warm, but heaven with age is cold.

> (*Ho ho, ho ho,*
> *The cloistered doubt*
> *Of olden times*
> *Is blurted out!*)

The Ancient of Days forever is young,
    Forever the scheme of Nature thrives;
I know a wind in purpose strong –
    It spins *against* the way it drives.
What if the gulfs their slimed foundations bare?
So deep must the stones be hurled
Whereon the throes of ages rear
The final empire and the happier world.

(*The poor old Past,*
The Future's slave,
She drudged through pain and crime
To bring about the blissful Prime,
Then — perished. There's *a grave!*)

    Power unanointed may come —
Dominion (unsought by the free)
    And the Iron Dome,
Stronger for stress and strain,
Fling her huge shadow athwart the main;
But the Founders' dream shall flee.
Age after age shall be
As age after age has been,
(From man's changeless heart their way they win);
And death be busy with all who strive —
Death, with silent negative.

        YEA AND NAY —
        EACH HATH HIS SAY;
        BUT GOD HE KEEPS THE MIDDLE WAY,
        NONE WAS BY
        WHEN HE SPREAD THE SKY;
        WISDOM IS VAIN, AND PROPHESY.

THE CRIME OF THE AGES
1861

       Poet, write!
Not of a purpose dark and dire,
That souls of evil fashion,
Nor the power that nerves the assassin's hand,
In the white heat of his passion:
       But let thy rhyme,
       Through every clime,
A burthen bear of this one crime:
Let the world draw in a shuddering breath,
Or the crime that aims at a nation's death!

       Minstrel, sing!
Not in affection's dulcet tone,
Or with sound of a soft recorder:
Strike not thy harp to a strain arranged
In measured, harmonic order:
       But loud and strong
       The notes prolong,
That thunder of a Nation's wrong;
Let a sound of war in thy notes appear,
Till the world opes wide a startled ear!

       Soldier, fight!
Thou hast a patriot's throbbing pulse,

And future history's pages,
Shall tell of the blood so freely shed
To redeem "the crime of the ages."
       Well may'st thou fight
       For Truth and Right,
And teach a rebel foe thy might!
Let a loyal heart, and undaunted will,
Show the world we are a Nation still!

       Prophet, speak!
Speak for the children of martyred sires,
An offspring the most ungrateful!
Warn them of Justice hurrying on,
To punish a deed so hateful!
       O read with thy
       Prophetic eye,
The omens of our troubled sky!
What is the picture beyond the gloom?
New life, new birth, or a Nation's tomb?

SHILOH
A Requiem

Skimming lightly, wheeling still,
    The swallows fly low
Over the field in clouded days,
    The forest-field of Shiloh –
Over the field where April rain
Solaced the parched ones stretched in pain
Through the pause of night
That followed the Sunday fight
    Around the church of Shiloh –
The church so lone, the log-built one,
That echoed to many a parting groan
      And natural prayer
    Of dying foemen mingled there –
Foemen at morn, but friends at eve –
    Fame or country least their care:
(What like a bullet can undeceive!)
    But now they lie low,
While over them the swallows skim,
    And all is hushed at Shiloh.

HERMAN MELVILLE

CHARLESTON

Calm as that second summer which precedes
    The first fall of the snow,
In the broad sunlight of heroic deeds,
    The City bides the foe.

As yet, behind their ramparts stern and proud,
    Her bolted thunders sleep –
Dark Sumter, like a battlemented cloud,
    Looms o'er the solemn deep.

No Calpe frowns from lofty cliff or scar
    To guard the holy strand;
But Moultrie holds in leash her dogs of war
    Above the level sand.

And down the dunes a thousand guns lie couched,
    Unseen, beside the flood –
Like tigers in some Orient jungle crouched
    That wait and watch for blood.

Meanwhile, through streets still echoing with trade,
    Walk grave and thoughtful men,
Whose hands may one day wield the patriot's blade
    As lightly as the pen.

And maidens, with such eyes as would grow dim
    Over a bleeding hound,
Seem each one to have caught the strength of him
    Whose sword she sadly bound.

Thus girt without and garrisoned at home,
    Day patient following day,
Old Charleston looks from roof, and spire, and dome,
    Across her tranquil bay.

Ships, through a hundred foes, from Saxon lands
    And spicy Indian ports,
Bring Saxon steel and iron to her hands,
    And Summer to her courts.

But still, along yon dim Atlantic line,
    The only hostile smoke
Creeps like a harmless mist above the brine,
    From some frail, floating oak.

Shall the Spring dawn, and she still clad in smiles,
    And with an unscathed brow,
Rest in the strong arms of her palm-crowned isles,
    As fair and free as now?

We know not; in the temple of the Fates
    God has inscribed her doom;
And, all untroubled in her faith, she waits
    The triumph or the tomb.

HENRY TIMROD   137

THE ARTILLERYMAN'S VISION

While my wife at my side lies slumbering, and the wars
    are over long,
And my head on the pillow rests at home, and the vacant
    midnight passes,
And through the stillness, through the dark, I hear, just
    hear, the breath of my infant,
There in the room as I wake from sleep this vision presses
    upon me;
The engagement opens there and then in fantasy unreal,
The skirmishers begin, they crawl cautiously ahead,
    I hear the irregular snap! snap!
I hear the sounds of the different missiles, the short *t-h-t!*
    t-h-t! of the rifle-balls,
I see the shells exploding leaving small white clouds,
    I hear the great shells shrieking as they pass,
The grape like the hum and whirr of wind through the
    trees, (tumultuous now the contest rages,)
All the scenes at the batteries rise in detail before me
    again,
The crashing and smoking, the pride of the men in their
    pieces,
The chief-gunner ranges and sights his piece and selects a
    fuse of the right time,
After firing I see him lean aside and look eagerly off to
    note the effect;

Elsewhere I hear the cry of a regiment charging, (the
    young colonel leads himself this time with brandish'd
    sword,)
I see the gaps cut by the enemy's volleys, (quickly fill'd up,
    no delay,)
I breathe the suffocating smoke, then the flat clouds hover
    low concealing all;
Now a strange lull for a few seconds, not a shot fired on
    either side,
Then resumed the chaos louder than ever, with eager calls
    and orders of officers,
While from some distant part of the field the wind wafts
    to my ears a shout of applause, (some special
    success,)
And ever the sound of the cannon far or near, (rousing
    even in dreams a devilish exultation and all the old
    mad joy in the depths of my soul,)
And ever the hastening of infantry shifting positions,
    batteries, cavalry, moving hither and thither,
(The falling, dying, I heed not, the wounded dripping and
    red I heed not, some to the rear are hobbling,)
Grime, heat, rush, aide-de-camps galloping by or on a full
    run,
With the patter of small arms, the warning of *s-s-t* of the
    rifles, (these in my vision I hear or see,)
And bombs bursting in air, and at night the vari-
    color'd rockets.

WALT WHITMAN   139

THE COLORED SOLDIERS

If the muse were mine to tempt it
    And my feeble voice were strong,
If my tongue were trained to measures,
    I would sing a stirring song.
I would sing a song heroic
    Of those noble sons of Ham,
Of the gallant colored soldiers
    Who fought for Uncle Sam!

In the early days you scorned them,
    And with many a flip and flout
Said "These battles are the white man's,
    And the whites will fight them out."
Up the hills you fought and faltered,
    In the vales you strove and bled,
While your ears still heard the thunder
    Of the foes' advancing tread.

Then distress fell on the nation,
    And the flag was drooping low;
Should the dust pollute your banner?
    No! the nation shouted, No!
So when War, in savage triumph,
    Spread abroad his funeral pall —
Then you called the colored soldiers,
    And they answered to your call.

And like hounds unleashed and eager
    For the life blood of the prey,
Sprung they forth and bore them bravely
    In the thickest of the fray.
And where'er the fight was hottest,
    Where the bullets fastest fell,
There they pressed unblanched and fearless
    At the very mouth of hell.

Ah, they rallied to the standard
    To uphold it by their might;
None were stronger in the labors,
    None were braver in the fight.
From the blazing beach of Wagner
    To the plains of Olustee,
They were foremost in the fight
    Of the battles of the free.

And at Pillow! God have mercy
    On the deeds committed there,
And the souls of those poor victims
    Sent to Thee without a prayer.
Let the fulness of Thy pity
    O'er the hot wrought spirits sway
Of the gallant colored soldiers
    Who fell fighting on that day!

Yes, the Blacks enjoy their freedom,
    And they won it dearly, too;
For the life blood of their thousands
    Did the southern fields bedew.
In the darkness of their bondage,
    In the depths of slavery's night,
Their muskets flashed the dawning,
    And they fought their way to light.

They were comrades then and brothers,
    Are they more or less to-day?
They were good to stop a bullet
    And to front the fearful fray.
They were citizens and soldiers,
    When rebellion raised its head;
And the traits that made them worthy, –
    Ah! those virtues are not dead.

They have shared your nightly vigils,
    They have shared your daily toil;
And their blood with yours commingling
    Has enriched the Southern soil.
They have slept and marched and suffered
    'Neath the same dark skies as you,
They have met as fierce a foeman,
    And have been as brave and true.

And their deeds shall find a record
    In the registry of Fame;
For their blood has cleansed completely
    Every blot of Slavery's shame.
So all honor and all glory
    To those noble sons of Ham —
The gallant colored soldiers
    Who fought for Uncle Sam!

PAUL LAURENCE DUNBAR   143

FOR THE UNION DEAD
Relinquunt Omnia Servare Rem Publicam.

The old South Boston Aquarium stands
in a Sahara of snow now. Its broken windows are
     boarded.
The bronze weathervane cod has lost half its scales.
The airy tanks are dry.

Once my nose crawled like a snail on the glass;
my hand tingled
to burst the bubbles
drifting from the noses of the cowed, compliant fish.

My hand draws back. I often sigh still
for the dark downward and vegetating kingdom
of the fish and reptile. One morning last March,
I pressed against the new barbed and galvanized

fence on the Boston Common. Behind their cage,
yellow dinosaur steamshovels were grunting
as they cropped up tons of mush and grass
to gouge their underworld garage.

Parking spaces luxuriate like civic
sandpiles in the heart of Boston.
A girdle of orange, Puritan-pumpkin colored girders
braces the tingling Statehouse,

shaking over the excavations, as it faces Colonel Shaw
and his bell-cheeked Negro infantry
on St. Gauden's shaking Civil War relief,
propped by a plank splint against the garage's
    earthquake.

Two months after marching through Boston,
half the regiment was dead;
at the dedication,
William James could almost hear the bronze Negroes
    breathe.

Their monument sticks like a fishbone
in the city's throat.
Its Colonel is as lean
as a compass-needle.

He has an angry wrenlike vigilance,
a greyhound's gentle tautness;
he seems to wince at pleasure,
and suffocate for privacy.

He is out of bounds now. He rejoices in man's lovely,
peculiar power to choose life and die –
when he leads his black soldiers to death,
he cannot bend his back.

On a thousand small town New England greens,
the old white churches hold their air

of sparse, sincere rebellion; frayed flags
quilt the graveyards of the Grand Army of the
     Republic.

The stone statues of the abstract Union Soldier
grow slimmer and younger each year –
wasp-waisted, they doze over muskets
and muse through their sideburns . . .

Shaw's father wanted no monument
except the ditch,
where his son's body was thrown
and lost with his "niggers."

The ditch is nearer.
There are no statues for the last war here;
on Boylston Street, a commercial photograph
shows Hiroshima boiling

over a Mosler Safe, the "Rock of Ages"
that survived the blast. Space is nearer.
When I crouch to my television set,
the drained faces of Negro school-children rise
     like balloons.

Colonel Shaw
is riding on his bubble,
he waits
for the blessèd break.

The Aquarium is gone. Everywhere,
giant finned cars nose forward like fish;
a savage servility
slides by on grease.

THE BLUE AND THE GRAY

"The women of Columbus, Mississippi, animated by nobler sentiments than are many of their sisters, have shown themselves impartial in their offerings made to the memory of the dead. They strewed flowers alike on the graves of the Confederate and of the National soldiers."

New York Tribune

By the flow of the inland river,
    Whence the fleets of iron have fled,
Where the blades of the grave-grass quiver,
    Asleep are the ranks of the dead; —
      Under the sod and the dew,
        Waiting the judgment day; —
      Under the one, the Blue;
        Under the other, the Gray.

These in the robings of glory,
    Those in the gloom of defeat,
All with the battle-blood gory,
    In the dusk of eternity meet; —
      Under the sod and the dew,
        Waiting the judgment day; —
      Under the laurel, the Blue;
        Under the willow, the Gray.

From the silence of sorrowful hours
    The desolate mourners go,
Lovingly laden with flowers
    Alike for the friend and the foe; —
        Under the sod and the dew,
            Waiting the judgment day; —
        Under the roses, the Blue;
            Under the lilies, the Gray.

So with an equal splendor
    The morning sun-rays fall,
With a touch, impartially tender,
    On the blossoms blooming for all;
        Under the sod and the dew,
            Waiting the judgment day; —
        Broidered with gold, the Blue;
            Mellowed with gold, the Gray.

So, when the Summer calleth,
    On forest and field of grain
With an equal murmur falleth
    The cooling drip of the rain; —
        Under the sod and the dew,
            Waiting the judgment day; —
        Wet with the rain, the Blue;
            Wet with the rain, the Gray.

Sadly, but not with upbraiding,
   The generous deed was done;
In the storm of the years that are fading,
   No braver battle was won; —
     Under the sod and the dew,
       Waiting the judgment day; —
     Under the blossoms, the Blue,
       Under the garlands, the Gray.

No more shall the war-cry sever,
   Or the winding rivers be red;
They banish our anger forever
   When they laurel the graves of our dead!
     Under the sod and the dew,
       Waiting the judgment day; —
     Love and tears for the Blue,
       Tears and love for the Gray.

WAR IS KIND

Do not weep, maiden, for war is kind.
Because your lover threw wild hands toward the sky
And the affrighted steed ran on alone,
Do not weep.
War is kind.

  Hoarse, booming drums of the regiment,
  Little souls who thirst for fight,
  These men were born to drill and die.
  The unexplained glory flies above them,
  Great is the Battle-God, great, and his Kingdom –
  A field where a thousand corpses lie.

Do not weep, babe, for war is kind.
Because your father tumbled in the yellow trenches,
Raged at his breast, gulped and died,
Do not weep.
War is kind.

  Swift blazing flag of the regiment,
  Eagle with crest of red and gold,
  These men were born to drill and die.
  Point for them the virtue of slaughter,
  Make plain to them the excellence of killing
  And a field where a thousand corpses lie.

Mother whose heart hung humble as a button
On the bright splendid shroud of your son,
Do not weep.
War is kind.

MODERN WARFARE:
WORLD WAR I

CHANNEL FIRING

That night your great guns, unawares,
Shook all our coffins as we lay,
And broke the chancel window-squares,
We thought it was the Judgment-day

And sat upright. While drearisome
Arose the howl of wakened hounds:
The mouse let fall the altar-crumb,
The worms drew back into the mounds,

The glebe cow drooled. Till God called, "No;
It's gunnery practice out at sea
Just as before you went below;
The world is as it used to be:

"All nations striving strong to make
Red war yet redder. Mad as hatters
They do no more for Christés sake
Than you who are helpless in such matters.

"That this is not the judgment-hour
For some of them's a blessed thing,
For if it were they'd have to scour
Hell's floor for so much threatening . . .

"Ha, ha. It will be warmer when
I blow the trumpet (if indeed
I ever do; for you are men,
And rest eternal sorely need)."

So down we lay again. "I wonder,
Will the world ever saner be,"
Said one, "than when He sent us under
In our indifferent century!"

And many a skeleton shook his head.
"Instead of preaching forty year,"
My neighbour Parson Thirdly said,
"I wish I had stuck to pipes and beer."

Again the guns disturbed the hour,
Roaring their readiness to avenge,
As far inland as Stourton Tower,
And Camelot, and starlit Stonehenge.

AUGUST 1914

What in our lives is burnt
In the fire of this?
The heart's dear granary?
The much we shall miss?

Three lives hath one life –
Iron, honey, gold.
The gold, the honey gone –
Left is the hard and cold.

Iron are our lives
Molten right through our youth.
A burnt space through ripe fields,
A fair mouth's broken tooth.

SHADOW

Here you are near me once more
Memories of my comrades dead in battle
Olive of time
Memories comprising now a single memory
As a hundred furs make only one coat
As those thousands of wounds make only one
      newspaper article
Impalpable dark appearance you have assumed
The changing form of my shadow
An Indian hiding in wait throughout eternity
Shadow you creep near me
But you no longer hear me
You will no longer know the divine poems I sing
But I hear you I see you still
Destinies
Multiple shadow may the sun watch over you
You who love me so much you will never leave me
You who dance in the sun without stirring the dust

              Shadow solar ink
              Handwriting of my light
              Caisson of regrets
              A god humbling himself

TRANSLATED BY ANNE HYDE GREET

LAMENT

Sleep and Death, the dark eagles
Rush all night long round this head:
The golden image of Man
Swallowed in the icy wave
Of eternity. On dreadful reefs
The crimson body shatters
And the dark voice mourns
Above the sea.
Sister of stormy dejection
Look, an anxious vessel
Sinks down beneath the stars,
The silent face of night.

GEORG TRAKL   159
TRANSLATED BY JOHN HOLLANDER

GRODEK

At evening the autumn forests
Resound with deadly weapons, golden plains
And blue lakes, above which the sun
Darkling unrolls; the night embraces
Dying warriors, the wild laments
Of their shattered mouths.
Yet silently in the willowed ground
A red cloud in which dwells an enraged god
Gathers. the spilled blood itself, lunar coolness;
All roads end up in black rot.
Beneath the golden boughs of night and stars
The sister's shadow flutters wavers through the silent
    wood
To greet the ghosts of the heroes, the bleeding heads;
And softly in the reeds sound the dark flutes of
    autumn.
Oh prouder sorrow! you brazen altars;
A mightier pain nourishes the hot flame of the spirit,
The grandchildren unborn.

       TRANSLATED BY JOHN HOLLANDER

TRUMPETS

Under pollarded willows, where brown children are
    playing
And leaves are driven, trumpets sound. A graveyard
    shudder.
Scarlet banners rush through the sadness of maples,
Cavalry riding by ryefields, and empty mills.

Or shepherds sing at night, and into the circle
Round their fire tread stags, the grove's old sorrow,
Dancers heave themselves up from the black wall.
Scarlet banners, laughter, blood, madness and
    trumpet-call.

GEORG TRAKL   161
TRANSLATED BY JOHN HOLLANDER

ON THE EASTERN FRONT

The wild organ of the winter storm
Is like the dark anger of the People,
The crimson surge of battle,
Of unleafed stars.

With broken brows, with silver arms
Night beckons to dying soldiers.
In the shade of the autumn ash-grove
The souls of the slain are sighing.

Thorny desert engirdles the town.
The moon chases frightened women
From bleeding steps.
Wild wolves broke through the gate.

TRANSLATED BY JOHN HOLLANDER

PATROL

The stones threaten
Window grins treachery
Branches strangle
Mountainous bushes rattle (rustle) off leaves
Shrieking
Death

WAR GRAVE

Stakes implore crossed arms
Writing dreads the pale unknown
Flowers insolent
Dusts timid
Glimmer
In tears
Luster
Oblivion

AUGUST STRAMM
TRANSLATED BY JOHN HOLLANDER

MAY, 1915

Let us remember Spring will come again
      To the scorched, blackened woods,
        where the wounded trees
  Wait with their old wise patience for the heavenly
    rain,
  Sure of the sky: sure of the sea to send its healing
    breeze,
      Sure of the sun. And even as to these
        Surely the Spring, when God shall please,
      Will come again like a divine surprise
To those who sit today with their great Dead, hands in
    their hands, eyes in their eyes,
At one with Love, at one with Grief: blind to the
    scattered things and changing skies.

THE DEAD

Blow out, you bugles, over the rich Dead!
   There's none of these so lonely and poor of old,
   But, dying, has made us rarer gifts than gold.
These laid the world away; poured out the red
Sweet wine of youth; gave up the years to be
   Of work and joy, and that unhoped serene,
   That men call age; and those who would have been,
Their sons, they gave, their immortality.

Blow, bugles, blow! They brought us, for our dearth,
   Holiness, lacked so long, and Love, and Pain.
Honour has come back, as a king, to earth,
   And paid his subjects with a royal wage;
And Nobleness walks in our ways again;
   And we have come into our heritage.

ROUEN
26 April–25 May 1915

Early morning over Rouen, hopeful, high, courageous
    morning,
And the laughter of adventure and the steepness of
    the stair,
And the dawn across the river, and the wind across
    the bridges,
And the empty littered station and the tired people there.

Can you recall those mornings and the hurry of
    awakening,
And the long-forgotten wonder if we should miss the way,
And the unfamiliar faces, and the coming of provisions,
And the freshness and the glory of the labour of the day?

Hot noontide over Rouen, and the sun upon the city,
Sun and dust unceasing, and the glare of cloudless skies,
And the voices of the Indians and the endless stream
    of soldiers,
And the clicking of the tatties, and the buzzing of the flies.

Can you recall those noontides and the reek of steam
    and coffee,
Heavy-laden noontides with the evening's peace to win,

And the little piles of Woodbines, and the sticky soda
     bottles,
And the crushes in the "Parlour", and the letters
     coming in?

Quiet night-time over Rouen, and the station full of
     soldiers,
All the youth and pride of England from the ends of all
     the earth;
And the rifles piled together, and the creaking of the
     sword-belts,
And the faces bent above them, and the gay, heart-
     breaking mirth.

Can I forget the passage from the cool white-bedded
     Aid Post
Past the long sun-blistered coaches of the khaki Red
     Cross train
To the truck train full of wounded, and the weariness
     and laughter,
And "Good-bye, and thank you, Sister", and the empty
     yards again?

Can you recall the parcels that we made them for the
     railroad,
Crammed and bulging parcels held together by their
     string,

And the voices of the sergeants who called the Drafts
    together,
And the agony and splendour when they stood to save
    the King?

Can you forget their passing, the cheering and the waving,
The little group of people at the doorway of the shed,
The sudden awful silence when the last train swung to
    darkness,
And the lonely desolation, and the mocking stars o'erhead?

Can you recall the midnights, and the footsteps of night
    watchers,
Men who came from darkness and went back to dark again,
And the shadows on the rail-lines and the all-inglorious
    labour,
And the promise of the daylight firing blue the window-
    pane?

Can you recall the passing through the kitchen door
    to morning,
Morning very still and solemn breaking slowly on
    the town,
And the early coastways engines that had met the
    ships at daybreak,
And the Drafts just out from England, and the
    day shift coming down?

Can you forget returning slowly, stumbling on the cobbles,
And the white-decked Red Cross barges dropping
      seawards for the tide,
And the search for English papers, and the blessed cool
      of water,
And the peace of half-closed shutters that shut out the
      world outside?

Can I forget the evenings and the sunsets on the island,
And the tall black ships at anchor far below our balcony,
And the distant call of bugles, and the white wine in
      the glasses,
And the long line of the street lamps, stretching
      Eastwards to the sea?

... When the world slips slow to darkness, when the office
      fire burns lower,
My heart goes out to Rouen, Rouen all the world away;
When other men remember I remember our Adventure
And the trains that go from Rouen at the ending of the day.

DULCE ET DECORUM EST

Bent double, like old beggars under sacks,
Knock-kneed, coughing like hags, we cursed through
    sludge,
Till on the haunting flares we turned our backs
And towards our distant rest began to trudge.
Men marched asleep. Many had lost their boots
But limped on, blood-shod. All went lame; all blind;
Drunk with fatigue; deaf even to the hoots
Of tired, outstripped Five-Nines that dropped behind.

Gas! GAS! Quick, boys! – An ecstasy of fumbling,
Fitting the clumsy helmets just in time;
But someone still was yelling out and stumbling,
And flound'ring like a man in fire or lime . . .
Dim, through the misty panes and thick green light,
As under a green sea, I saw him drowning.
In all my dreams, before my helpless sight,
He plunges at me, guttering, choking, drowning.

If in some smothering dreams you too could pace
Behind the wagon that we flung him in,
And watch the white eyes writhing in his face,
His hanging face, like a devil's sick of sin;
If you could hear, at every jolt, the blood
Come gargling from the froth-corrupted lungs,

Obscene as cancer, bitter as the cud
Of vile, incurable sores on innocent tongues, –
My friend, you would not tell with such high zest
To children ardent for some desperate glory,
The old Lie: Dulce et decorum est
Pro patria mori.

STRANGE MEETING

It seemed that out of battle I escaped
Down some profound dull tunnel, long since scooped
Through granites which titanic wars had groined.

Yet also there encumbered sleepers groaned,
Too fast in thought or death to be bestirred.
Then, as I probed them, one sprang up, and stared
With piteous recognition in fixed eyes,
Lifting distressful hands, as if to bless.
And by his smile, I knew that sullen hall, –
By his dead smile I knew we stood in Hell.
With a thousand pains that vision's face was grained;
Yet no blood reached there from the upper ground,
And no guns thumped, or down the flues made moan.
"Strange friend," I said, "here is no cause to mourn."
"None," said that other, "save the undone years,
The hopelessness. Whatever hope is yours,
Was my life also; I went hunting wild
After the wildest beauty in the world,
Which lies not calm in eyes, or braided hair,
But mocks the steady running of the hour,
And if it grieves, grieves richlier than here.
For by my glee might many men have laughed,
And of my weeping something had been left,
Which must die now. I mean the truth untold,

The pity of war, the pity war distilled.
Now men will go content with what we spoiled,
Or, discontent, boil bloody, and be spilled.
They will be swift with swiftness of the tigress.
None will break ranks, though nations trek from
    progress.
Courage was mine, and I had mystery,
Wisdom was mine, and I had mastery:
To miss the march of this retreating world
Into vain citadels that are not walled.
Then, when much blood had clogged their
    chariot-wheels,
I would go up and wash them from sweet wells,
Even with truths that lie too deep for taint.
I would have poured my spirit without stint
But not through wounds; not on the cess of war.
Foreheads of men have bled where no wounds were.

"I am the enemy you killed, my friend.
I knew you in this dark: for so you frowned
Yesterday through me as you jabbed and killed.
I parried; but my hands were loath and cold.
Let us sleep now . . ."

BREAK OF DAY IN THE TRENCHES

The darkness crumbles away.
It is the same old druid Time as ever,
Only a live thing leaps my hand,
A queer sardonic rat,
As I pull the parapet's poppy
To stick behind my ear.
Droll rat, they would shoot you if they knew
Your cosmopolitan sympathies.
Now you have touched this English hand
You will do the same to a German
Soon, no doubt, if it be your pleasure
To cross the sleeping green between.
It seems you inwardly grin as you pass
Strong eyes, fine limbs, haughty athletes,
Less chanced than you for life,
Bonds to the whims of murder,
Sprawled in the bowels of the earth,
The torn fields of France.
What do you see in our eyes
At the shrieking iron and flame
Hurled through still heavens?
What quaver – what heart aghast?
Poppies whose roots are in man's veins
Drop, and are ever dropping;
But mine in my ear is safe –
Just a little white with the dust.

ISAAC ROSENBERG

THE REAR-GUARD
(*Hindenburg Line, April 1917*)

Groping along the tunnel, step by step,
He winked his prying torch with patching glare
From side to side, and sniffed the unwholesome air.

Tins, boxes, bottles, shapes too vague to know,
A mirror smashed, the mattress from a bed;
And he, exploring fifty feet below
The rosy gloom of battle overhead.

Tripping, he grabbed the wall; saw some one lie
Humped at his feet, half-hidden by a rug,
And stooped to give the sleeper's arm a tug.
"I'm looking for headquarters." No reply.
"God blast your neck!" (For days he'd had no sleep,)
"Get up and guide me through this stinking place."
Savage, he kicked a soft, unanswering heap,
And flashed his beam across the livid face
Terribly glaring up, whose eyes yet wore
Agony dying hard ten days before;
And fists of fingers clutched a blackening wound.

Alone he staggered on until he found
Dawn's ghost that filtered down a shafted stair
To the dazed, muttering creatures underground

Who hear the boom of shells in muffled sound.
At last, with sweat of horror in his hair,
He climbed through darkness to the twilight air
Unloading hell behind him step by step.

FIELD AMBULANCE IN RETREAT
Via Dolorosa, Via Sacra

A straight flagged road, laid on the rough earth,
A causeway of stone from beautiful city to city,
Between the tall trees, the slender, delicate trees,
Through the flat green land, by plots of flowers, by
      black canals thick with heat.

The road-makers made it well
Of fine stone, strong for the feet of the oxen and of the
      great Flemish horses,
And for the high wagons piled with corn from the
      harvest.
And the labourers are few;
They and their quiet oxen stand aside and wait
By the long road loud with the passing of the guns, the
      rush of armoured cars, and the tramp of an army
      on the march forward to battle;
And, where the piled corn-wagons went, our dripping
      Ambulance carries home
Its red and white harvest from the fields.

The straight flagged road breaks into dust, into a thin
      white cloud,
About the feet of a regiment driven back league by
      league,

Rifles at trail, and standards wrapped in black funeral
   cloths.
Unhasting, proud in retreat,
They smile as the Red Cross Ambulance rushes by.
(You know nothing of beauty and of desolation who
   have not seen
That smile of an army in retreat.)
They go: and our shining, beckoning danger goes
   with them,
And our joy in the harvests that we gathered in at
   nightfall in the fields;
And like an unloved hand laid on a beating heart
Our safety weighs us down.
Safety hard and strange; stranger and yet more hard
As, league after dying league, the beautiful, desolate
   Land
Falls back from the intolerable speed of an Ambulance
   in retreat
On the sacred, dolorous Way.

AN IRISH AIRMAN FORESEES
HIS DEATH

I know that I shall meet my fate
Somewhere among the clouds above;
Those that I fight I do not hate,
Those that I guard I do not love;
My country is Kiltartan Cross,
My countrymen Kiltartan's poor,
No likely end could bring them loss
Or leave them happier than before.
Nor law, nor duty bade me fight,
Nor public men, nor cheering crowds,
A lonely impulse of delight
Drove to this tumult in the clouds;
I balanced all, brought all to mind,
The years to come seemed waste of breath,
A waste of breath the years behind
In balance with this life, this death.

MADEMOISELLE FROM ARMENTIÈRES

Madamoiselle from Armentiers, parley voo,
Madamoiselle from Armentiers, parley voo,
  Madamoiselle from Armentiers,
  She hasn't been kissed in forty years,
Hinky, dinky, parley voo.

Madamoiselle from Armentiers, parley voo,
Madamoiselle from Armentiers, parley voo,
  She had a form like the back of a hack,
  When she cried the tears ran down her back,
Hinky, dinky, parley voo.

Madamoiselle from Armentiers, parley voo,
Madamoiselle from Armentiers, parley voo,
  She never could hold the love of a man
  'Cause she took her baths in a talcum can,
Hinky, dinky, parley voo.

Madamoiselle from Armentiers, parley voo,
Madamoiselle from Armentiers, parley voo,
  She had four chins, her knees would knock,
  And her face would stop a coo-coo clock.
Hinky, dinky, parley voo.

Madamoiselle from Armentiers, parley voo,
Madamoiselle from Armentiers, parley voo,
   She could guzzle a barrel of sour wine,
   And eat a hog without peeling the rine,
Hinky, dinky, parley voo.

Madamoiselle from Armentiers, parley voo,
Madamoiselle from Armentiers, parley voo,
   She could beg a franc, a drink, a meal,
   But it wasn't because of sex appeal,
Hinky, dinky, parley voo.

The M.P.'s think they won the war, parley voo,
The M.P.'s think they won the war, parley voo,
   The M.P.'s think they won the war
   By standing guard at a café door,
Hinky, dinky, parley voo.

The officers get the pie and cake, parley voo,
The officers get the pie and cake, parley voo,
   The officers get the pie and cake,
   And all we get is the bellyache,
Hinky, dinky, parley voo.

The sergeant ought to take a bath, parley voo,
The sergeant ought to take a bath, parley voo,
   If he ever changes his underwear

The frogs will give him a croix de guerre,
Hinky, dinky, parley voo.

You might forget the gas and shells, parley voo,
You might forget the stinking hells, parley voo,
    You might forget the groans and yells,
    But you'll never forget the madamoiselles,
Hinky, dinky, parley voo.

Madamoiselle from Armentiers, parley voo,
Madamoiselle from Armentiers, parley voo,
    Just blow your nose and dry your tears
    For we'll be back in a few short years.
Hinky, dinky, parley voo.

AS THE TEAM'S HEAD BRASS

As the team's head brass flashed out on the turn
The lovers disappeared into the wood.
I sat among the boughs of the fallen elm
That strewed an angle of the fallow, and
Watched the plough narrowing a yellow square
Of charlock. Every time the horses turned
Instead of treading me down, the ploughman leaned
Upon the handles to say or ask a word,
About the weather, next about the war.
Scraping the share he faced towards the wood,
And screwed along the furrow till the brass flashed
Once more.
          The blizzard felled the elm whose crest
I sat in, by a woodpecker's round hole,
The ploughman said. "When will they take it away?"
"When the war's over." So the talk began –
One minute and an interval of ten,
A minute more and the same interval.
"Have you been out?" "No." "And don't want to,
      perhaps?"
"If I could only come back again, I should.
I could spare an arm. I shouldn't want to lose
A leg. If I should lose my head, why, so,
I should want nothing more . . . Have many gone
From here?" "Yes." "Many lost?" "Yes, a good few.

Only two teams work on the farm this year.
One of my mates is dead. The second day
In France they killed him. It was back in March,
The very night of the blizzard, too. Now if
He had stayed here we should have moved the tree."
"And I should not have sat here. Everything
Would have been different. For it would have been
Another world." "Ay, and a better, though
If we could see all all might seem good." Then
The lovers came out of the wood again:
The horses started and for the last time
I watched the clods crumble and topple over
After the ploughshare and the stumbling team.

THE VETERAN
May, 1916

We came upon him sitting in the sun,
    Blinded by war, and left. And past the fence
There came young soldiers from the Hand and Flower,
    Asking advice of his experience.

And he said this, and that, and told them tales,
    And all the nightmares of each empty head
Blew into air; then, hearing us beside,
    "Poor chaps, how'd they know what it's like?"
      he said.

And we stood there, and watched him as he sat,
    Turning his sockets where they went away,
Until it came to one of us to ask
    "And you're – how old?"
        "Nineteen, the third of May."

IN FLANDERS FIELDS

In Flanders fields the poppies blow
Between the crosses, row on row,
    That mark our place; and in the sky
    The larks, still bravely singing, fly
Scarce heard amid the guns below.

We are the Dead. Short days ago
We lived, felt dawn, saw sunset glow,
    Loved and were loved, and now we lie
        In Flanders fields.

Take up our quarrel with the foe:
To you from failing hands we throw
    The torch; be yours to hold it high.
    If ye break faith with us who die
We shall not sleep, though poppies grow
        In Flanders fields.

RECALLING WAR

Entrance and exit wounds are silvered clean,
The track aches only when the rain reminds.
The one-legged man forgets his leg of wood,
The one-armed man his jointed wooden arm.
The blinded man sees with his ears and hands
As much or more than once with both his eyes.
Their war was fought these twenty years ago
And now assumes the nature-look of time,
As when the morning traveller turns and views
His wild night-stumbling carved into a hill.

What, then, was war? No mere discord of flags
But an infection of the common sky
That sagged ominously upon the earth
Even when the season was the airiest May.
Down pressed the sky, and we, oppressed, thrust out
Boastful tongue, clenched fist and valiant yard.
Natural infirmities were out of mode,
For Death was young again: patron alone
Of healthy dying, premature fate-spasm.

Fear made fine bed-fellows. Sick with delight
At life's discovered transitoriness,
Our youth became all-flesh and waived the mind.
Never was such antiqueness of romance,

Such tasty honey oozing from the heart.
And old importances came swimming back –
Wine, meat, log-fires, a roof over the head,
A weapon at the thigh, surgeons at call.
Even there was a use again for God –
A word of rage in lack of meat, wine, fire,
In ache of wounds beyond all surgeoning.

War was return of earth to ugly earth,
War was foundering of sublimities,
Extinction of each happy art and faith
By which the world had still kept head in air.
Protesting logic or protesting love,
Until the unendurable moment struck –
The inward scream, the duty to run mad.

And we recall the merry ways of guns –
Nibbling the walls of factory and church
Like a child, piecrust; felling groves of trees
Like a child, dandelions with a switch!
Machine-guns rattle toy-like from a hill,
Down in a row the brave tin-soldiers fall:
A sight to be recalled in elder days
When learnedly the future we devote
To yet more boastful visions of despair.

WORLD WAR II
AND AFTER

TO MARGOT HEINEMANN

Heart of the heartless world,
Dear heart, the thought of you
Is the pain at my side,
The shadow that chills my view.

The wind rises in the evening,
Reminds that autumn's near.
I am afraid to lose you,
I am afraid of my fear.

On the last mile to Huesca,
The last fence for our pride,
Think so kindly, dear, that I
Sense you at my side.

And if bad luck should lay my strength
Into the shallow grave,
Remember all the good you can;
Don't forget my love.

JOHN CORNFORD

NAMING OF PARTS

Today we have naming of parts. Yesterday,
We had daily cleaning. And tomorrow morning,
We shall have what to do after firing. But today,
Today we have naming of parts. Japonica
Glistens like coral in all of the neighbouring gardens,
     And today we have naming of parts.

This is the lower sling swivel. And this
Is the upper sling swivel, whose use you will see,
When you are given your slings. And this is the piling
     swivel,
Which in your case you have not got. The branches
 Hold in the gardens their silent, eloquent gestures,
     Which in our case we have not got.

This is the safety-catch, which is always released
With an easy flick of the thumb. And please do not let me
See anyone using his finger. You can do it quite easy
If you have any strength in your thumb. The blossoms
Are fragile and motionless, never letting anyone see
     Any of them using their finger.

And this you can see is the bolt. The purpose of this
Is to open the breech, as you see. We can slide it

Rapidly backwards and forwards: we call this
Easing the spring. And rapidly backwards and
      forwards
The early bees are assaulting and fumbling the flowers:
      They call it easing the Spring.

They call it easing the Spring: it is perfectly easy
If you have any strength in your thumb: like the bolt,
And the breech, and the cocking-piece, and the point
      of balance,
Which in our case we have not got; and the almond-
      blossom
Silent in all of the gardens and the bees going
      backwards and forwards,
      For today we have naming of parts.

HENRY REED   195

1 SEPTEMBER 1939

The first, scattering rain on the Polish cities.
That afternoon a man squat' on the shore
Tearing a square of shining cellophane.
Some easily, some in evident torment tore,
Some for a time resisted, and then burst.
All this depended on fidelity . . .
One was blown out and borne off by the waters,
The man was tortured by the sound of rain.

Children were sent from London in the morning
But not the sound of children reached his ear.
He found a mangled feather by the lake,
Lost in the destructive sand this year
Like feathery independence, hope. His shadow
Lay on the sand before him, under the lake
As under the ruined library our learning.
The children play in the waves until they break.

The Bear crept under the Eagle's wing and lay
Snarling; the other animals showed fear,
Europe darkened its cities. The man wept,
Considering the light which had been there,
The feathered gull against the twilight flying.
As the little waves ate away the shore
The cellophane, dismembered, blew away.
The animals ran, the Eagle soared and dropt.

HITLER SPRING

Né quella ch'a veder lo sol si gira ...

Dante (?) to Giovanni Quirini

Dense, the white cloud of moths whirling
crazily around the feeble streetlights and parapets
strews on the pavement a shroud that crunches
    like sugar
underfoot; now the looming summer frees
the night frost held
in the dead season's dungeon caves
among the gardens stepping from Maiano down to
    these sandbanks here.

Minutes past a demon angel zoomed down the street
through aisles of heiling assassins; suddenly a
    Hellmouth yawned, lurid,
draped with hooked crosses, seized him, gulped
    him down;
the shops are bolted shut, humble
inoffensive windows, but armed, even they,
with howitzers and wargame toys;
the shop is shuttered now where the butcher stood
wreathing muzzles of slaughtered goats with berries
    and flowers,
the holiday of gentle killers ignorant of blood
becomes a loathsome shindy of shattered wings,

197

ghosts on the wet mud, water gnawing
at the banks, and no one's guiltless anymore.

All for nothing then? – and the Roman
candles in San Giovanni slowly blanching
the horizon, and the vows, and the long farewells
strong as any christening in the sad, sullen waiting
for the horde (but a jewel furrowed the air, dropping
Tobias's angels, all seven, on the icefloes and rivers
of your shores, sowing them
with the future), and the sun-seeking flowers sprouting
from your hands – all scorched, sucked dry
by pollen hissing like fire, stinging
like wind-whipped snow . . .
                                        O this wounded
Spring is still a day of feasting, if only its frost could kill
this death at last! Look, Clizia, look up,
on high, it's your fate, you
who preserve through change unchanging love,
until the blind sunlight you bear within you
goes dark in the Other, consuming itself
in Him, for all men. Perhaps even now the sirens,
the bells pealing their salute to the monsters in
      the night
of their hellish Halloween, are blending

with the sound that, heaven-loosed, comes down
    to conquer –
and with it comes the breathing of a dawn that
    will shine
tomorrow for us all, white light but no wings
of terror, on the burnt-out wadis of the south.

IN WESTMINSTER ABBEY

Let me take this other glove off
    As the *vox humana* swells,
And the beauteous fields of Eden
    Bask beneath the Abbey bells.
Here, where England's statesmen lie,
Listen to a lady's cry.

Gracious Lord, oh bomb the Germans.
    Spare their women for Thy Sake,
And if that is not too easy
    We will pardon Thy Mistake.
But, gracious Lord, whate'er shall be,
Don't let anyone bomb me.

Keep our Empire undismembered
    Guide our Forces by Thy Hand,
Gallant blacks from far Jamaica,
    Honduras and Togoland;
Protect them Lord in all their fights,
And, even more, protect the whites.

Think of what our Nation stands for,
    Books from Boot's and country lanes,
Free speech, free passes, class distinction,
    Democracy and proper drains.

Lord, put beneath Thy special care
One-eighty-nine Cadogan Square.

Although dear Lord I am a sinner,
    I have done no major crime;
Now I'll come to Evening Service
    Whensoever I have the time.
So, Lord, reserve for me a crown,
And do not let my shares go down.

I will labour for Thy Kingdom,
    Help our lads to win the war,
Send white feathers to the cowards
    Join the Women's Army Corps,
Then wash the Steps around Thy Throne
In the Eternal Safety Zone.

Now I feel a little better,
    What a treat to hear Thy Word,
Where the bones of leading statesmen,
    Have so often been interr'd.
And now, dear Lord, I cannot wait
Because I have a luncheon date.

HOW TO KILL

Under the parabola of a ball,
a child turning into a man,
I looked into the air too long.
The ball fell in my hand, it sang
in the closed fist: *Open Open*
Behold a gift designed to kill.

Now in my dial of glass appears
the soldier who is going to die.
He smiles, and moves about in ways
his mother knows, habits of his.
The wires touch his face: I cry
NOW. Death, like a familiar, hears

and look, has made a man of dust
of a man of flesh. This sorcery
I do. Being damned, I am amused
to see the centre of love diffused
and the waves of love travel into vacancy.
How easy it is to make a ghost.

The weightless mosquito touches
her tiny shadow on the stone,
and with how like, how infinite
a lightness, man and shadow meet.
They fuse. A shadow is a man
when the mosquito death approaches.

RECONCILIATION

All day beside the shattered tank he'd lain
Like a limp creature hacked out of its shell,
Now shrivelling on the desert's grid,
Now floating above a sharp-set ridge of pain.

There came a roar, like water, in his ear.
The mortal dust was laid. He seemed to be lying
In a cool coffin of stone walls,
While memory slid towards a plunging weir.

The time that was, the time that might have been
Find in this shell of stone a chance to kiss
Before they part eternally:
He feels a world without, a world within

Wrestle like old antagonists, until each is
Balancing each. Then, in a heavenly calm,
The lock gates open, and beyond
Appear the argent, swan-assemblied reaches.

C. DAY LEWIS   203

GALLANTRY

The Colonel in a casual voice
spoke into the microphone a joke
which through a hundred earphones broke
into the ears of a doomed race.

Into the ears of the doomed boy, the fool
whose perfectly mannered flesh fell
in opening the door for a shell
as he had learnt to do at school.

Conrad luckily survived the winter:
he wrote a letter to welcome
the auspicious spring: only his silken
intentions severed with a single splinter.

Was George fond of little boys?
We always suspected it,
but who will say: since George was hit
we never mention our surmise.

It was a brave thing the Colonel said,
but the whole sky turned too hot
and the three heroes never heard what
it was, gone deaf with steel and lead.

But the bullets cried with laughter,
the shells were overcome with mirth,
plunging their heads in steel and earth –
(the air commented in a whisper).

THE FURY OF AERIAL BOMBARDMENT

You would think the fury of aerial bombardment
Would rouse God to relent; the infinite spaces
Are still silent. He looks on shock-pried faces.
History, even, does not know what is meant.

You would feel that after so many centuries
God would give man to repent; yet he can kill
As Cain could, but with multitudinous will,
No farther advanced than in his ancient furies.

Was man made stupid to see his own stupidity?
Is God by definition indifferent, beyond us all?
Is the eternal truth man's fighting soul
Wherein the Beast ravens in its own avidity?

Of Van Wettering I speak, and Averill,
Names on a list, whose faces I do not recall
But they are gone to early death, who late in school
Distinguished the belt feed lever from the belt
        holding pawl.

THE DEATH OF THE BALL TURRET GUNNER

From my mother's sleep I fell into the State,
And I hunched in its belly till my wet fur froze.
Six miles from earth, loosed from its dream of life,
I woke to black flak and the nightmare fighters.
When I died they washed me out of the turret
        with a hose.

LOSSES

It was not dying: everybody died.
It was not dying: we had died before
In the routine crashes – and our fields
Called up the papers, wrote home to our folks,
And the rates rose, all because of us.
We died on the wrong page of the almanac,
Scattered on mountains fifty miles away;
Diving on haystacks, fighting with a friend,
We blazed up on the lines we never saw.
We died like aunts or pets or foreigners.
(When we left high school nothing else had died
For us to figure we had died like.)

In our new planes, with our new crews, we bombed
The ranges by the desert or the shore,
Fired at towed targets, waited for our scores –
And turned into replacements and woke up
One morning, over England, operational.
It wasn't different: but if we died
It was not an accident but a mistake
(But an easy one for anyone to make).
We read our mail and counted up our missions –
In bombers named for girls, we burned
The cities we had learned about in school –
Till our lives wore out; our bodies lay among

The people we had killed and never seen.
When we lasted long enough they gave us medals;
When we died they said, "Our casualties were low."
They said, "Here are the maps"; we burned the cities.

It was not dying – no, not ever dying;
But the night I died I dreamed that I was dead,
And the cities said to me: "Why are you dying?
We are satisfied, if you are; but why did I die?"

CARRIER

She troubles the waters, and they part and close
    Like a people tired of an old queen
Who has made too many progresses; and so she goes.
Leisurely swift her passage between green
    South islands; careful and helpless through
      the locks;
At lazy anchor huge and peacock vain.
On the streaked sea at dawn she stands to the streaks
    And when her way and the wind have made
      her long,
The planes rise heavy from her whining deck.
Then the bomb's luck, the gun's poise and chattering.
    The far-off dying, are her near affair;
With her sprung creatures become weak or strong
    She watches them down the sky and disappear,
    Heart gone, sea-bound, committed all to air.

CARENTAN O CARENTAN

Trees in the old days used to stand
And shape a shady lane
Where lovers wandered hand in hand
Who came from Carentan.

This was the shining green canal
Where we came two by two
Walking at combat-interval.
Such trees we never knew.

The day was early June, the ground
Was soft and bright with dew.
Far away the guns did sound,
But here the sky was blue.

The sky was blue, but there a smoke
Hung still above the sea
Where the ships together spoke
To towns we could not see.

Could you have seen us through a glass
You would have said a walk
Of farmers out to turn the grass,
Each with his own hay-fork.

The watchers in their leopard suits
Waited till it was time,
And aimed between the belt and boot
And let the barrel climb.

I must lie down at once, there is
A hammer at my knee.
And call it death or cowardice,
Don't count again on me.

Everything's all right, Mother,
Everyone gets the same
At one time or another.
It's all in the game.

I never strolled, nor ever shall,
Down such a leafy lane.
I never drank in a canal,
Nor ever shall again.

There is a whistling in the leaves
And it is not the wind,
The twigs are falling from the knives
That cut men to the ground.

Tell me, Master-Sergeant,
The way to turn and shoot.
But the Sergeant's silent
That taught me how to do it.

O Captain, show us quickly
Our place upon the map.
But the Captain's sickly
And taking a long nap.

Lieutenant, what's my duty,
My place in the platoon?
He too's a sleeping beauty,
Charmed by that strange tune.

Carentan O Carentan
Before we met with you
We never yet had lost a man
Or known what death could do.

LOUIS SIMPSON   213

FIRST SNOW IN ALSACE

The snow came down last night like moths
Burned on the moon; it fell till dawn,
Covered the town with simple cloths.

Absolute snow lies rumpled on
What shellbursts scattered and deranged,
Entangled railings, crevassed lawn.

As if it did not know they'd changed,
Snow smoothly clasps the roofs of homes
Fear-gutted, trustless and estranged.

The ration stacks are milky domes;
Across the ammunition pile
The snow has climbed in sparkling combs.

You think: beyond the town a mile
Or two, this snowfall fills the eyes
Of soldiers dead a little while.

Persons and persons in disguise,
Walking the new air white and fine,
Trade glances quick with shared surprise.

At children's windows, heaped, benign,
As always, winter shines the most,
And frost makes marvellous designs.

The night guard coming from his post,
Ten first-snows back in thought, walks slow
And warms him with a boyish boast:

He was the first to see the snow.

NIGHT OF BATTLE

Europe: 1944
as regarded from a great distance

Impersonal the aim
Where giant movements tend;
Each man appears the same;
Friend vanishes from friend.

In the long path of lead
That changes place like light
No shape of hand or head
Means anything tonight.

Only the common will
For which explosion spoke;
And stiff on field and hill
The dark blood of the folk.

I WANT TO DIE IN MY OWN BED

All night the army came up from Gilgal
To get to the killing field, and that's all.
In the ground, warp and woof, lay the dead.
I want to die in my own bed.

Like slits in a tank, their eyes were uncanny,
I'm always the few and they are the many.
I must answer. They can interrogate my head.
But I want to die in my own bed.

The sun stood still in Gibeon. Forever so, it's willing
To illuminate those waging battle and killing.
I may not see my wife when her blood is shed,
But I want to die in my own bed.

Samson, his strength in his long black hair,
My hair they sheared off when they made me a hero
Perforce, and taught me to charge ahead.
I want to die in my own bed.

I saw you could live and furnish with grace
Even a lion's maw, if you've got no other place.
I don't even mind to die alone, to be dead,
But I want to die in my own bed.

YEHUDA AMICHAI   217
TRANSLATED BY BENJAMIN AND BARBARA
HARSHAV

HOW MUCH LONGER?

Day after day after day it goes on
and no one knows how to stop it or escape.
Friends come bearing impersonal agonies,
I hear our hopeless laughter, I watch us drink.
War is in everyone's eyes, war is made
in the kitchen, in the bedroom, in the car at stoplights.
A marriage collapses like a burning house
and the other houses smolder. Old friends
make their way in silence. Students stare
at their teachers, and suddenly feel afraid.
The old people are terrified like cattle
rolling their eyes and bellowing, while the young
wander in darkness, dazed, half-believing
some half-forgotten poem, or else come out
with their hearts on fire, alive in the last days.
Small children roam the neighborhoods armed
with submachineguns, gas masks and riot sticks.
Excavations are made in us and slowly
we are filled in with used-up things: knives
too dull to cut bread with, bombs that failed to go off,
cats smashed on the highway, broken pencils,
slivers of soap, hair, gristle, old TV sets
that hum and stare out blindly like the insane.
Bridges kneel down, the cities billow and plunge
like horses in their smoke, the tall buildings

open their hysterical burning eyes at night,
the leafy suburbs look up at the clouds and tremble –
and my wife leaves her bed before dawn, walking
the icy pasture, shrieking her grief to the cows,
praying in tears to the softening blackness. I hear her
outside the window, crazed, inconsolable,
and go out to fetch her. Yesterday she saw
a photograph, Naomi our little girl
in a ditch in Viet Nam, half in the water,
the rest of her, beached on the mud, was horribly
        burned.

NEWSREEL

This would not be the war we fought in. See, the
foliage is heavier, there were no hills of that size there.

But I find it impossible not to look for actual persons
known to me and not seen since; impossible not to look
for myself.

The scenery angers me, I know there is something
wrong, the sun is too high, the grass too trampled, the
peasants' faces too broad, and the main square of the
capital had no arcades like those.

Yet the dead look right, and the roofs of the huts, and
the crashed fuselage burning among the ferns.

But this is not the war I came to see, buying my ticket,
stumbling through the darkness, finding my place
among the sleepers and masturbators in the dark.

I thought of seeing the General who cursed us, whose
name they gave to an expressway; I wanted to see the
faces of the dead when they were living.

Once I know they filmed us, back at the camp behind
the lines, taking showers under the trees and showing
pictures of our girls.

Somewhere there is a film of the war we fought in, and it must contain the flares, the souvenirs, the shadows of the netted brush, the standing in line of the innocent, the hills that were not of this size.

Somewhere my body goes taut under the deluge, somewhere I am naked behind the lines, washing my body in the water of that war.

Someone has that war stored up in metal canisters, a memory he cannot use, somewhere my innocence is proven with my guilt, but this would not be the war I fought in.

"COME ON, COME BACK"
(*incident in a future war*)

Left by the ebbing tide of battle
On the field of Austerlitz
The girl soldier Vaudevue sits
Her fingers tap the ground, she is alone
At midnight in the moonlight she is sitting alone on a
    round flat stone

Graded by the Memel Conference first
Of all humane exterminators
M.L.5.
Has left her just alive
Only her memory is dead for evermore.
She fears and cries, Ah me why am I here?
Sitting alone on a round flat stone on a hummock
    there.

Rising, staggering, over the ground she goes
Over the seeming miles of rutted meadow
To the margin of a lake
The sand beneath her feet
Is cold and damp and firm to the waves' beat.

Quickly – as a child, an idiot, as one without memory –
She strips her uniform off, strips, stands and plunges

Into the icy waters of the adorable lake.
On the surface of the water lies
A ribbon of white moonlight
The waters on either side of the moony track
Are black as her mind.
Her mind is as secret from her
As the water on which she swims,
As secret as profound as ominous.

Weeping bitterly for her ominous mind, her plight
Up the river of white moonlight she swims
Until a treacherous undercurrent
Seizing her in an icy-amorous embrace
Dives with her, swiftly severing
The waters which close above her head.

An enemy sentinel
Finding the abandoned clothes
Waits for the swimmer's return
("Come on, come back")
Waiting, whiling away the hour
Whittling a shepherd's pipe from the hollow reeds.

In the chill light of dawn
Ring out the pipe's wild notes
"Come on, come back."

Vaudevue
In the swift and subtle current's close embrace
Sleeps on, stirs not, hears not the familiar tune
Favourite of all the troops of all the armies
Favourite of Vaudevue
For she had sung it too
Marching to Austerlitz,
"Come on, come back."

GENERAL
OBSERVATIONS

IN RESPONSE TO HORACE'S CLAIM
THAT IT IS LOVELY AND FITTING
TO DIE FOR ONE'S COUNTRY

Pro patria mori dulce et
Decorum est
But for both you and your country
To live is best.

John Owen

WAR
from Queen Mab

War is the statesman's game, the priest's delight,
The lawyer's jest, the hired assassin's trade,
And, to those royal murderers, whose mean thrones
Are bought by crimes of treachery and gore,
The bread they eat, the staff on which they lean.
Guards, garbed in blood-red livery, surround
Their palaces, participate the crimes
That force defends, and from a nation's rage
Secure the crown, which all the curses reach
That famine, frenzy, woe and penury breathe.
These are the hired bravos who defend
The tyrant's throne – the bullies of his fear:
These are the sinks and channels of worst vice,
The refuse of society, the dregs
Of all that is most vile: their cold hearts blend
Deceit with sternness, ignorance with pride,
All that is mean and villainous, with rage
Which hopelessness of good, and self-contempt,
Alone might kindle; they are decked in wealth,
Honour and power, then are sent abroad
To do their work. The pestilence that stalks
In gloomy triumph through some eastern land
Is less destroying. They cajole with gold,
And promises of fame, the thoughtless youth

Already crushed with servitude: he knows
His wretchedness too late, and cherishes
Repentance for his ruin, when his doom
Is sealed in gold and blood!
Those too the tyrant serve, who, skilled to snare
The feet of justice in the toils of law,
Stand, ready to oppress the weaker still;
And, right or wrong, will vindicate for gold,
Sneering at public virtue, which beneath
Their pityless tread lies torn and trampled, where
Honour sits smiling at the sale of truth.

WARNINGS UNHEEDED

plato told

him: he couldn't
believe it (jesus

told him; he
wouldn't believe
it) lao

tsze
certainly told
him, and general
(yes

mam)
sherman;
and even
(believe it
or

not) you
told him: i told
him; we told him
(he didn't believe it, no

sir) it took
a nipponized bit of
the old sixth

avenue
el; in the top of his head: to tell

him

LEAD!

Hail, holy Lead! – of human feuds the great
   And universal arbiter; endowed
   With penetration to pierce any cloud
Fogging the field of controversial hate,
And with a swift, inevitable, straight,
   Searching precision find the unavowed
   But vital point. Thy judgment, when allowed
By the chirurgeon, settles the debate.
O useful metal! – were it not for thee
   We'd grapple one another's ears alway:
But when we hear thee buzzing like a bee
   We, like old Muhlenberg, "care not to stay."
And when the quick have run away like pullets
Jack Satan smelts the dead to make new bullets.

WHAT THE BULLET SANG

O joy of creation
        To be!
O rapture to fly
        And be free!
Be the battle lost or won,
   Though its smoke shall hide the sun,
I shall find my love, – the one
        Born for me!

I shall know him where he stands,
        All alone,
With the power in his hands
        Not o'erthrown;
I shall know him by his face,
   By his godlike front and grace;
I shall hold him for a space,
        All my own!

It is he – O my love!
        So bold!
It is I – all thy love
        Foretold!
It is I. O love! what bliss!
   Dost thou answer to my kiss?
O sweetheart! what is this
        Lieth there so cold?

ON THE DANGER OF WAR

Avert, High Wisdom, never vainly wooed,
This threat of War, that shows a land brain-sick
When nations gain the pitch where rhetoric
Seems reason they are ripe for cannon's food.
Dark looms the issue though the cause be good,
But with the doubt 'tis our old devil's trick.
O now the down-slope of the lunatic
Illumine lest we redden of that brood.
For not since man in his first view of thee
Ascended to the heavens giving sign
Within him of deep sky and sounded sea,
Did he unforfeiting thy laws transgress;
In peril of his blood his ears incline
To drums whose loudness is their emptiness.

GEORGE MEREDITH

SOLDIERS' SONG
from "For the Time Being"

When the Sex War ended with the slaughter of the
        Grandmothers,
They found a bachelor's baby suffocating under them;
Somebody called him George and that was the end of
        it:
        They hitched him up to the Army.
        George, you old debutante,
        How did you get in the Army?

In the Retreat from Reason he deserted on his rocking-
        horse
And lived on a fairy's kindness till he tired of kicking
        her;
He smashed her spectacles and stole her cheque-book
        and mackintosh
        Then cruised his way back to the Army.
        George, you old numero,
        How did you get in the Army?

Before the Diet of Sugar he was using razor-blades
And exited soon after with an allergy to maidenheads;
He discovered a cure of his own, but no one would
        patent it,
        So he showed up again in the Army.

George, you old flybynight,
How did you get in the Army?

When the Vice Crusades were over he was hired by
     some Muscovites
Prospecting for deodorants among the Eskimos;
He was caught by a common cold and
                  condemned to the whiskey mines,
    But schemozzled back to the Army.
    George, you old Emperor,
    How did you get in the Army?

Since Peace was signed with Honour he's been
    minding his business;
But, whoops, here comes His Idleness, buttoning his
    uniform;
Just in tidy time to massacre the Innocents;
    He's come home to roost in the Army.
    George, you old matador,
    Welcome back to the Army.

W. H. AUDEN

SONG FOR A FALLEN WARRIOR
(*Blackfeet*)

O my son, farewell!
You have gone beyond the great river,
Your spirit is on the other side of the Sand Buttes;
I will not see you for a hundred winters;
You will scalp the enemy in the green prairie,
Beyond the great river.
When the warriors of the Blackfeet meet,
When they smoke the medicine-pipe and dance the
     war-dance,
They will ask, "Where is Isthumaka? –
Where is the bravest of the Mannikappi?"
He fell on the war-path.
     Mai-ram-bo, mai-ram-bo.

Many scalps will be taken for your death;
The Crows will lose many horses;
Their women will weep for their braves,
They will curse the spirit of Isthumaka.

O my son! I will come to you
And make moccasins for the war-path,
As I did when you struck the lodge
Of the "Horse-Guard" with the tomahawk.
Farewell, my son! I will see you
Beyond the broad river.
     Mai-ram-bo, mai-ram-bo.

236 ANON.
    TRANSLATED BY JOHN MASON BROWNE

THE MAN HE KILLED

"Had he and I but met
        By some old ancient inn,
We should have sat us down to wet
        Right many a nipperkin!

"But ranged as infantry,
        And staring face to face,
I shot at him as he at me,
        And killed him in his place.

"I shot him dead because –
        Because he was my foe,
Just so: my foe of course he was;
        That's clear enough; although

"He thought he'd 'list, perhaps,
        Off-hand like – just as I –
Was out of work – had sold his traps –
        No other reason why.

"Yes; quaint and curious war is!
        You shoot a fellow down
You'd treat if met where any bar is,
        Or help to half-a-crown."

THOMAS HARDY

TWO ARMIES

Deep in the winter plain, two armies
Dig their machinery, to destroy each other.
Men freeze and hunger. No one is given leave
On either side, except the dead, and wounded.
These have their leave; while new battalions wait
On time at last to bring them violent peace.

All have become so nervous and so cold
That each man hates the cause and distant words
That brought him here, more terribly than bullets.
Once a boy hummed a popular marching song,
Once a novice hand flapped their salute;
The voice was choked, the lifted hand fell,
Shot through the wrist by those of his own side.

From their numb harvest, all would flee, except
For discipline drilled once in an iron school
Which holds them at the point of the revolver.
Yet when they sleep, the images of home
Ride wishing horses of escape
Which herd the plain in a mass unspoken poem.

Finally, they cease to hate: for although hate
Bursts from the air and whips the earth with hail
Or shoots it up in fountains to marvel at,
And although hundreds fall, who can connect
The inexhaustible anger of the guns
With the dumb patience of those tormented animals?

Clean silence drops at night, when a little walk
Divides the sleeping armies, each
Huddled in linen woven by remote hands.
When the machines are stilled, a common suffering
Whitens the air with breath and makes both one
As though these enemies slept in each other's arms.

Only the lucid friend to aerial raiders
The brilliant pilot moon, stares down
Upon this plain she makes a shining bone
Cut by the shadows of many thousand bones.
Where amber clouds scatter on No-Man's-Land
She regards death and time throw up
The furious words and minerals which destroy.

STEPHEN SPENDER   239

RECRUITING DRIVE

Under the willow the willow
   I heard the butcher-bird sing,
Come out you fine young fellow
   From under your mother's wing.
I'll show you the magic garden
   That hangs in the beamy air,
The way of the lynx and the angry Sphinx
   And the fun of the freezing fair.

Lie down lie down with my daughter
   Beneath the Arabian tree,
Gaze on your face in the water
   Forget the scribbling sea.
Your pillow the nine bright shiners,
   Your bed the spilling sand,
But the terrible toy of my lily-white boy
   Is the gun in his innocent hand.

You must take off your clothes for the doctor,
   And stand as straight as a pin,
His hand of stone on your white breast-bone
   Where the bullets all go in.
They'll dress you in lawn and linen
   And fill you with Plymouth gin,
O the devil may wear a rose in his hair
   I'll wear my fine doe-skin.

My mother weeps as I leave her
    But I tell her it won't be long,
The murderers wail in Wandsworth Gaol
    But I shoot a more popular song.
Down in the enemy country
    Under the enemy tree
There lies a lad whose heart has gone bad
    Waiting for me, for me.

He says I have no culture
    And that when I've stormed the pass
I shall fall on the farm with a smoking arm
    And ravish his bonny lass.
Under the willow the willow
    Death spreads her dripping wings
And caught in the snare of the bleeding air
    The butcher-bird sings, sings, sings.

CAPTAIN IN TIME OF PEACE

Crudely continues what has been begun
Crudely, because the crude expedient
Sets crude and final what is to be won.
Tactics commit me falsely, what I want
Is not the raising of a siege but this:
    Honour in the town at peace.

I see you bend your head by the fireplace
Softly examining your outspread hand,
A puzzled look unguarded on your face,
As if you did not fully understand.
How can I with most gentleness explain
    I will not plot my moves again?

Something I try, and yet when I express
Trite cinema endearments, all is said.
There, I think still in terms of mere success
– Success in raising up your downturned head.
Pity a lumpish soldier out of work,
    And teach him manners with a look.

And if I cannot gracefully receive
When you are generous, know that the habit
Of soldiers is to loot. So please forgive
All my inadequacy: I was fit
For peaceful living once, and was not born
    A clumsy brute in uniform.

ANOTHER KIND OF WAR

Soldier, there is a war between the mind
And sky, between thought and day and night. It is
For that the poet is always in the sun,

Patches the moon together in his room
To his Virgilian cadences, up down,
Up down. It is a war that never ends.

Yet it depends on yours. The two are one.
They are a plural, a right and left, a pair,
Two parallels that meet if only in

The meeting of their shadows or that meet
In a book in a barrack, a letter from Malay.
But your war ends. And after it you return

With six meats and twelve wines or else without
To walk another room . . . Monsieur and comrade,
The soldier is poor without the poet's lines,

His petty syllabi, the sounds that stick,
Inevitably modulating, in the blood.
And war for war, each has its gallant kind.

How simply the fictive hero becomes the real;
How gladly with proper words the soldier dies,
If he must, or lives on the bread of faithful speech.

WALLACE STEVENS   243

ACKNOWLEDGMENTS

Thanks are due to the following copyright holders for their permission to reprint:

AMICHAI, YEHUDA: 'I Want to Die in My Own Bed' by Yehuda Amichai from *A Life of Poetry*, translated by Benjamin and Barbara Harshav. Published by HarperCollins.

APOLLINAIRE, GUILLAUME: 'Shadow' by Guillaume Apollinaire, translated by Anne Hyde Greet. Reprinted by permission of The University of California Press.

AUDEN, W. H.: 'Soldiers' Song' from *W. H. Auden Collected Poems* by W. H. Auden, edited by Edward Mendelson. Copyright © 1944 and 1972 by W. H. Auden. Reprinted by permission of Random House, Inc.

BERRYMAN, JOHN: '1 September 1939' from *Collected Poems 1937–1971* by John Berryman. Copyright © 1989 by Kate Donahue Berryman. Reprinted by permission of Farrar, Straus and Giroux, LLC.

BETJEMAN, JOHN: 'In Westminster Abbey' by John Betjeman from *Collected Poems*. Reprinted by permission of John Murray.

CANNAN, MAY WEDDERBURN: 'Rouen'. First published by B. H. Blackwell, 1917. Copyright © Mr. James C. Slater.

CAUSLEY, CHARLES: 'Recruiting Drive' from *Collected Poems* by Charles Causley. Copyright © MacMillan. Reprinted by permission of David Higham Associates.

CORNFORD, JOHN: 'To Margot Heinemann' from *Understand the Weapon* by John Cornford. Reprinted by permission of Carcanet Press Ltd. All rights reserved.

CUMMINGS, E. E.: 'Plato told' is reprinted from *Complete Poems 1904–1962* by E. E. Cummings, edited by George J. Firmage, by permission of W. W. Norton & Company. Copyright © 1991 by the Trustees for the E. E. Cummings Trust and George James Firmage.

DAY LEWIS, C.: 'Reconciliation' from *Collected Poems* by C. Day Lewis, published by Sinclair-Stevenson (1992). Copyright © 1992 in this edition The Estate of C. Day Lewis.

245

DOUGLAS, KEITH: 'How to Kill' and 'Gallantry' from *The Collected Poems of Keith Douglas*. Published by Faber & Faber. Copyright © J. C. Hall.

EBERHART, RICHARD: 'The Fury of Aerial Bombardment' from *Collected Poems 1930–1986* by Richard Eberhart. Copyright © 1960, 1976, 1987 by Richard Eberhart. Used by permission of Oxford University Press.

GRAVES, ROBERT: 'Recalling War' from *Complete Poems* by Robert Graves. Reprinted by permission of Carcanet Press Ltd. All rights reserved.

GUNN, THOM: 'Captain in Time of Peace' from *Collected Poems* by Thom Gunn. Copyright © 1994 by Thom Gunn. Reprinted by permission of Farrar, Straus and Giroux, LLC.

HALL, DONALD: 'O Flodden Field' from *Old and New Poems* by Donald Hall. Copyright © 1990 by Donald Hall. Reprinted by permission of Houghton Mifflin Company. All rights reserved.

HA-NAGID, SHMUEL: 'First War' from *Selected Poems*, translated by Peter Cole. Published by Princeton University Press.

HORACE: 'After the Battle of Actium' from *The Odes and Epodes of Horace*, translated by Joseph P. Clancy. Reprinted by permission of The University of Chicago Press.

HORACE: 'Dulce et Decorum est pro Patria Mori', translated by James Michie. Reprinted by permission of the translator.

JARRELL, RANDALL: 'Losses' and 'The Death of the Ball Turret Gunner' from *The Complete Poems* by Randall Jarrell. Copyright © 1969 and copyright renewed © 1997 by Mary van S. Jarrell. Reprinted by permission of Farrar, Straus and Giroux, LLC.

KAO, CH'I: 'Lament of a Soldier's Wife' from *Sunflower Splendour* by Ch'i Kao, translated by Irving Y. Lo. Reprinted by permission of Wu-Chi-Liu.

KIPLING, RUDYARD: 'After the Rebellion' and 'Danny Deever' from *Rudyard Kipling's Verse*. Reprinted by permission of A. P. Watt.

LERMONTOV, MIKHAIL: 'The Dream' from *Major Poetic Works* by Mikhail Lermontov, translated by Anatoly Liberman. Published by The University of Minnesota Press. Reprinted by permission of Anatoly Liberman.

246

MEREDITH, WILLIAM: 'Carrier' from *Ships and Other Figures* by William Meredith. Published by Princeton University Press. Rights reverted to the author.

MEW, CHARLOTTE: 'May, 1915' from *Collected Poems and Selected Prose* by Charlotte Mew. Reprinted by permission of Carcanet Press Ltd. All rights reserved.

MEZEY, ROBERT: 'How Much Longer?' from *The Door Standing Open* by Robert Mezey. Rights reverted to the author. Reprinted by permission of Robert Mezey.

MICKIEWICZ, ADAM: 'The Year 1812' by Adam Mickiewicz, translated by Donald Davie from *Collected Poems*. Published by Carcanet Press, reprinted by permission of Doreen Davie, widow of the deceased poet.

MONTALE, EUGENIO: 'Hitler Spring' from *The Storm and Other Things* by Eugenio Montale, translated by William Arrowsmith. Reprinted by permission of Arnoldo Mondadori Editore.

MUIR, EDWIN: 'Ballad of Hector in Hades' from *Collected Poems* by Edwin Muir. Copyright © 1960 by Willa Muir. Used by permission of Oxford University Press, Inc.

REED, HENRY: 'Naming of Parts' from *A Map of Verona* by Henry Reed, Jonathan Cape, Random House (UK) Ltd.

RICH, ADRIENNE: 'Newsreel' (#9 from 'Shooting Script') by Adrienne Rich from *A Will to Change*. Published by W. W. Norton & Co. Reprinted by permission of Adrienne Rich.

SASSOON, SIEGFRIED: 'The Rear-guard' from *Collected Poems*. Published by Faber & Faber. Copyright © George Sassoon.

SIMPSON, LOUIS: 'Carentan O Carentan' from *A Dream of Governors*. Rights reverted to the author.

SINCLAIR, MAY: 'Field Ambulance in Retreat' by May Sinclair. Reproduced by permission of Curtis Brown Ltd., London, on behalf of the Estate of May Sinclair. Copyright © The Estate of May Sinclair.

SMITH, STEVIE: 'Come on, Come back' by Stevie Smith, from *The Collected Poems of Stevie Smith*. Copyright © 1972 by Stevie Smith. Reprinted by permission of New Directions Corp.

SPENDER, STEPHEN: 'Two Armies' from *Collected Poems 1928–1953* by

Stephen Spender. Reprinted by permission of Random House, Inc.

STEVENS, WALLACE: 'Another Kind of War' from *Collected Poems* by Wallace Stevens. Copyright 1954 by Wallace Stevens. Reprinted by permission of Alfred A. Knopf, Inc.

WILBUR, RICHARD: 'First Snow in Alsace' from *The Beautiful Changes and Other Poems*. Copyright 1947 and renewed 1975 by Richard Wilbur, reprinted by permission of Harcourt, Inc.

WINTERS, YVOR: 'Night of Battle' from *Collected Poems*, edited by Donald Davie. Reprinted with the permission of Ohio University Press/Swallow Press, Athens, Ohio.

YEATS, W. B.: 'An Irish Airman Forsees his Death' from *Collected Poems*. Reprinted by permission of A. P. Watt.

Although every effort has been made to trace and contact copyright holders, in a few instances this has not been possible. If notified, the publishers will be pleased to rectify any omission in future editions.

INDEX OF AUTHORS

252

253

254